Coming to grips with malaria in the new millennium

Lead authors
Awash Teklehaimanot, Coordinator
Burt Singer, Coordinator
Andrew Spielman
Yeşim Tozan
Allan Schapira

UN Millennium Project
Task Force on HIV/AIDS, Malaria, TB,
and Access to Essential Medicines
Working Group on Malaria
2005

EARTHSCAN

London • Sterling, Va.

First published by Earthscan in the UK and USA in 2005

ISBN: 1-84407-226-6 paperback

For a full list of publications please contact:

Earthscan
8–12 Camden High Street
London, NW1 0JH, UK
Tel: +44 (0)20 7387 8558
Fax: +44 (0)20 7387 8998
Email: earthinfo@earthscan.co.uk
Web: www.earthscan.co.uk
22883 Quicksilver Drive, Sterling, VA 20166-2012, USA

Earthscan is an imprint of James and James (Science Publishers) Ltd and publishes in association with the International Institute for Environment and Development

A catalogue record for this book is available from the British Library

Library of Congress Cataloging-in-Publication Data

A catalog record has been requested

Coventry University

This publication should be cited as: UN Millennium Project 2005. *Coming to Grips with Malaria in the New Millennium*. Task Force on HIV/AIDS, Malaria, TB, and Access to Essential Medicines, Working Group on Malaria.

Photos: Front cover Giacomo Pirozzi/UNICEF; back cover, top to bottom, Christopher Dowswell/UNDP, Pedro Cote/UN, Giacomo Pirozzi/Panos Pictures, Liba Taylor/Panos Pictures, Jørgen Schytte/UNDP, UN Photo Library Giacomo Pirozzi/UNICEF, Curt Carnemark/World Bank, Pedro Cote/UN, Franck Charton/UNICEF, Paul Chesley/Getty Images, Ray Witlin/World Bank, Pete Turner/Getty Images.

This book was edited, designed, and produced by Communications Development Inc., Washington, D.C., and its UK design partner, Grundy & Northedge.

The Millennium Project was commissioned by the UN Secretary-General and sponsored by the UN Development Group, which is chaired by the Administrator of the United Nations Development Programme. The report is an independent publication that reflects the views of the members of the Task Force on HIV/AIDS, Malaria, TB, and Access to Essential Medicines, Working Group on Malaria, who contributed in their personal capacity. This publication does not necessarily reflect the views of the United Nations, the United Nations Development Programme, or their Member States.

Printed on elemental chlorine-free paper

Foreword

The world has an unprecedented opportunity to improve the lives of billions of people by adopting practical approaches to meeting the Millennium Development Goals. At the request of the UN Secretary-General Kofi Annan, the UN Millennium Project has identified practical strategies to eradicate poverty by scaling up investments in infrastructure and human capital while promoting gender equality and environmental sustainability. These strategies are described in the UN Millennium Project's report *Investing in Development: A Practical Plan to Achieve the Millennium Development Goals*, which was coauthored by the coordinators of the UN Millennium Project task forces.

The task forces have identified the interventions and policy measures needed to achieve each of the Goals. In *Coming to Grips with Malaria in the New Millennium*, the Working Group on Malaria of the Task Force on HIV/ AIDS, Malaria, TB, and Access to Essential Medicines proposes an operational framework for scaling up integrated packages of effective antimalarial interventions with the aim of improving health nationally while also promoting economic development locally—an emphasis that is echoed in *Investing in Development*. An integral part of this framework is building stronger national health systems as a platform for delivering essential antimalarial and other health commodities and services. This report highlights the importance of free provision of insecticide-treated bednets, application of residual insecticides, and provision of effective antimalarial medicines and diagnostics to those at risk of malaria. Adequate information systems for health and effective management skills at all levels of the health system are paramount to effectively allocating resources, monitoring program performance, and evaluating the extent to which the health-related Millennium Development Goals are realized.

Funding for malaria control remains far below the $2–$3 billion require per year to achieve the desired impact. Closing this resource gap is, howeve possible with the combined efforts of donor nations and endemic countries.

This report has been prepared by a group of leading experts who contrib uted in their personal capacity and volunteered their time to this importar task. I am very grateful for their thorough and skilled efforts and I am sure tha the practical options for action in this report will make an important contribu tion to achieving the Millennium Development Goals. I strongly recommen it to anyone who is interested in the role of malaria control within a compre hensive development framework.

Jeffrey D. Sack
New Yor
January 17, 200

Contents

Maps

Tables

Working group members

Task force coordinators

Awash Teklehaimanot, Professor of Clinical Epidemiology, Mailman School of Public Health and Center for Global Health and Economic Development, The Earth Institute at Columbia University, United States

Burt Singer, Charles and Marie Robertson Professor of Public and International Affairs, Woodrow Wilson School of Public and International Affairs, Princeton University, United States

Members of the Working Group on Malaria

James Banda, Senior Advisor, Roll Back Malaria Partnership Secretariat, World Health Organization, Switzerland

Chris Hentschel, Chief Executive Officer, Medicines for Malaria Venture, Switzerland

Kamini Mendis, Senior Advisor, Roll Back Malaria Department, World Health Organization, Switzerland

Maria Veronicah Mugisha, Director, Epidemiology and Public Hygiene, Ministry of Health, Rwanda

José Ribeiro, Head, Section of Medical Entomology, Laboratory of Malaria and Vector Research, National Institute of Allergy and Infectious Diseases, National Institutes of Health, United States

Allan Schapira, Coordinator, Roll Back Malaria Department, World Health Organization, Switzerland

Brian Sharp, Director, Malaria Research Program, Medical Research Council, South Africa

Andrew Spielman, Professor of Tropical Public Health, Department of Immunology and Infectious Diseases, Harvard School of Public Health, Harvard University, United States

Marcel Tanner, Director, Swiss Tropical Institute, Professor of Epidemiology and Public Health at the University of Basel, Switzerland

Yeya Touré, Manager, Steering Committee for Molecular Entomology, Malaria Research Coordinator, Special Programme for Research and Training in Tropical Diseases–World Health Organization, Switzerland

Task force associate

Yeşim Tozan, Postdoctoral Fellow, Center for Global Health and Economic Development, The Earth Institute at Columbia University, United States

Preface

The Millennium Declaration, adopted by world leaders at the United Nations Millennium Summit in September 2000, formed the basis for eight mutually supportive goals known as the Millennium Development Goals. Originating in a series of United Nations resolutions and agreements over the past decade, the Goals are intended to resolve the most important structural constraints impeding sustainable economic growth and hence social progress in developing countries. This concerted effort is directed at changing the course of policy in several key areas at all necessary levels to combat poverty, disease, illiteracy, gender inequality, and environmental degradation, particularly in the poorest and most vulnerable populations. For countries trapped in entrenched poverty, the Millennium Development Goals have highlighted health as a priority investment area in view of the fact that any progress on this front is mutually reinforcing and also contributes to better outcomes in the other Goals.

The Monterrey Consensus, adopted by a large group of countries at the International Conference on Financing for Development in 2000, elicited the commitment of countries to create an equitable global economic system by providing more extensive debt relief and improved market access to poor countries. This commitment is necessary to achieve the Millennium Development Goals.

The UN Millennium Project aims to identify the best strategies and the resources needed to achieve the Millennium Development Goals in all developing countries by the year 2015. To this end, 10 task forces have been established, each composed of scholars, policymakers, and practitioners from developed and developing countries affiliated with UN agencies, civil society organizations, public agencies, nongovernmental organizations, and private sector institutions. The task forces divided this work according to their expertise with the aim of consolidating synergies among the Goals to achieve an integrated strategy by the year 2005. The UN Millennium Project Task Force on HIV/AIDS, Malaria, TB, and Access to Essential Medicines aims to devise a framework for accelerated implementation of strategies for achieving Millennium Development Goal 6: "Combat HIV/AIDS, malaria and other diseases." It has four working groups focusing on these three diseases and access to essential medicines.

The Working Group on Malaria puts forward a global plan for scaling up country-level malaria activities and makes a number of recommendations that require priority action to achieve the working group's proposed target on malaria: "Reduce malaria morbidity and mortality by 75 percent by 2015 from the 2005 baseline level." A range of effective tools and interventions exist for the prevention, treatment, and control of malaria. However, coverage levels are unacceptably low in endemic countries. More importantly, interventions are not reaching those who need them most.

This report identifies key implementation challenges and resources required for accelerated implementation of integrated packages of effective antimalaria interventions designed to improve health nationally while also promoting economic development locally. The task force members agree that the public good will best be served by the free provision of insecticide-treated nets, application of residual insecticides, and provision of effective antimalarial medicines and diagnostics. An integral part of this global plan is building stronger national health systems as a platform for delivering essential antimalarial commodities and effective interventions to those at risk of malaria. Adequate health information systems and effective management skills are paramount to sustainable disease control efforts. Finally, a program of applied and basic research is required to develop a series of alternative medicines and insecticides, rapid and reliable diagnostic tools suitable for field use, and appropriate vaccines.

This document is intended for the governments of affected countries, donor nations, the private sector agencies, nongovernmental foundations, civil society organizations, nongovernmental organizations, and academic and research institutes. The task force members hope that this document will provide a useful framework for action and will stimulate an immediate response to the plight of people living in malaria-endemic areas.

Acknowledgments

The Working Group on Malaria gratefully acknowledges the comments and contributions of external commentators on this document, Joel Breman, Chris Curtis, and Hailay Desta Teklehaimanot.

We thank Anthony Kiszewski for developing the global costs of malaria; Margaret Kruk for reviewing the document and providing extensive comments; Anne Mills and Sammy Shillcutt for providing the global costs of malaria; Bernard Nahlen for contributing to an earlier draft on monitoring and evaluation; Asnake Kebede, Ambachew Medhin, and Amir Said for conducting the needs assessment and costing of malaria control in Ethiopia; and Don de Savigny, Morteza Zaim, and Stephen Zebiak for their comments and suggestions in the early drafting of the document.

Charles Delacollette, Marina Gavrioushkina, Asefaw Getachew, Anne Guilloux, Natasha Morris, Rindra Randremanana, and Milijaona Randrianarivelojosia provided the figures used in the document. Albert Cho, Michael Krouse, Rohit Wanchoo, and Alice Wiemers provided valuable assistance and support from the secretariat of the UN Millennium Project. Daniel Eiras and Nima Tabloei provided excellent research assistance. Ingrid Peterson contributed to the editing of a few sections in the document. Melody Corry provided excellent administrative support to the Working Group on Malaria.

The report was edited and produced by Meta de Coquereaumont, Bruce Ross-Larson, Hope Steele, Christopher Trott, and Elaine Wilson of Communications Development Incorporated.

Abbreviations

ACT	artemisinin-based combination therapy
AIDS	acquired immunodeficiency syndrome
CGIAR	Consultative Group on International Agricultural Research
DDT	dichlorodiphenyltrichloroethane
DHS	Demographic and Health Surveys
DSS	Demographic Surveillance Systems
GFATM	Global Fund to Fight AIDS, Tuberculosis, and Malaria
GIS	geographic information systems
GPS	global positioning system
HIS	health information systems
HIV	human immunodeficiency virus
IMCI	Integrated Management of Childhood Illness
IPTi	Intermittent Preventive Treatment in Infants
IRRI	International Rice Research Institute
IWMI	International Water Management Institute
MICS	Multiple Indicator Cluster Survey
MIM	Multilateral Initiative on Malaria
MIS	Malaria Indicator Survey
MMV	Medicines for Malaria Venture
NGO	nongovernmental organization
NMCP	National Malaria Control Program
OPID	Opération de Pulvérisation Intra Domiciliaire
PHAP	Public Health Action Plan
RBM	Roll Back Malaria initiative
SIMA	Systemwide Initiative on Malaria and Agriculture
SP	sulfadoxine-pyrimethamine
TB	tuberculosis

TEHIP	Tanzanian Essential Health Interventions Project
TRIPS	Trade-Related Aspects of Intellectual Property Rights
WHO	World Health Organization

Millennium Development Goals

Goal 1

Eradicate extreme poverty and hunger

Target 1.
Halve, between 1990 and 2015, the proportion of people whose income is less than $1 a day

Target 2.
Halve, between 1990 and 2015, the proportion of people who suffer from hunger

Goal 2

Achieve universal primary education

Target 3.
Ensure that, by 2015, children everywhere, boys and girls alike, will be able to complete full course of primary schooling

Goal 3

Promote gender equality and empower women

Target 4.
Eliminate gender disparity in primary and secondary education, preferably by 2005, and all levels of education no later than 2015

Goal 4

Reduce child mortality

Target 5.
Reduce by two-thirds, between 1990 and 2015, the under-five mortality rate

Goal 5

Improve maternal health

Target 6.
Reduce by three-quarters, between 1990 and 2015, the maternal mortality ratio

Goal 6

Combat HIV/AIDS, malaria, and other diseases

Target 7.
Have halted by 2015 and begun to reverse the spread of HIV/AIDS

Target 8.
Have halted by 2015 and begun to reverse the incidence of malaria and other major disease

Goal 7

Ensure environmental sustainability

Target 9.

Integrate the principles of sustainable development into country policies and programs and reverse the loss of environmental resources

Target 10.

Halve, by 2015, the proportion of people without sustainable access to safe drinking water and basic sanitation

Target 11.

Have achieved by 2020 a significant improvement in the lives of at least 100 million slum dwellers

Goal 8

Develop a global partnership for development

Target 12.

Develop further an open, rule-based, predictable, nondiscriminatory trading and financial system (includes a commitment to good governance, development, and poverty reduction—both nationally and internationally)

Target 13.

Address the special needs of the Least Developed Countries (includes tariff- and quota-free access for Least Developed Countries' exports, enhanced program of debt relief for heavily indebted poor countries [HIPCs] and cancellation of official bilateral debt, and more generous official development assistance for countries committed to poverty reduction)

Target 14.

Address the special needs of landlocked developing countries and small island developing states (through the Program of Action for the Sustainable Development of Small Island Developing States and 22nd General Assembly provisions)

Target 15.

Deal comprehensively with the debt problems of developing countries through national and international measures in order to make debt sustainable in the long term

Target 16.

In cooperation with developing countries, develop and implement strategies for decent and productive work for youth

Target 17.

In cooperation with pharmaceutical companies, provide access to affordable essential drugs in developing countries

Target 18.

In cooperation with the private sector, make available the benefits of new technologies, especially information and communications technologies

Executive summary

Malaria is a major global health problem; more than 50 percent of the world's population is exposed to the disease. An exact assessment of the extent of malaria's health burden is fraught with formidable challenges. The disease is estimated to cause 300–500 million episodes of acute illness and 1.1–2.7 million deaths worldwide every year. More than 90 percent of the world's malaria burden is in Africa. Malaria takes its greatest toll on young children and pregnant women. At least 20 percent of all childhood deaths in Sub-Saharan Africa can be attributed to the disease. Pregnant women are at great risk of malaria infection and may suffer a range of complications from anemia to cerebral malaria. These complications also affect the survival and development of their newborns.

Malaria control has been increasingly recognized as an integral part of a comprehensive development framework with a key role in poverty reduction. The disease has been estimated to reduce economic growth by more than one percentage point a year in highly endemic countries. The perceived risk of infection has been suggested to negatively affect decisions related to investment, trade, and crop choice and to impose sizeable longer term costs by slowing economic growth in malarious countries and widening the gap between them and the rest of the world. Malaria exacts its toll on agricultural communities and households living in rural tropical areas where subsistence economy persists. The malaria transmission season generally coincides with that of planting or harvesting. As a result, a brief period of illness that delays planting or coincides with harvesting may cause catastrophic economic effects in the world's poorest regions, deepening the impoverishment of rural agricultural households through direct output and income losses.

In the decades following the Global Malaria Eradication Program (1955–69) the geographic range of the disease contracted substantially, and political

Very few health gains have translated into sustained societal improvements in the lives of those living in malaria-endemic areas

commitment and resources allocated for malaria control and research dwindled. Malaria became a disease of the poor nations situated mainly in tropical areas, and malaria control programs degraded significantly or were abandoned entirely in afflicted countries. Since the 1980s and 1990s, the malaria conundrum has been exacerbated by the development and spread of resistance to effective and affordable antimalarial medicines and insecticides and by the general weakening of health systems. The situation is compounded by the frequent occurrence of epidemics and complex emergencies.

Following the global resurgence of the disease, the Roll Back Malaria (RBM) initiative was launched in 1998 by the World Health Organization in partnership with the World Bank, the United Nations Children's Fund, and the United Nations Development Programme. RBM has been instrumental in creating global awareness and political commitment for malaria control. Both malaria-endemic countries and the international donor community expressed their readiness to embark on sustainable control efforts at a national scale. However, five years after launching the RBM initiative, country-level implementation of malaria control efforts has been severely limited because of a lack of resources for large-scale procurement of essential health commodities such as antimalarials, insecticide-treated nets, and insecticides. The growing HIV/AIDS pandemic has also overstretched the already limited resources available for malaria prevention and control in the past decade, particularly in Africa.

Overall, despite a series of declarations on malaria, pledges by global partners, and advances in the development of antimalarial tools over the past five decades, very few health gains have translated into sustained societal improvements in the lives of those living in endemic areas, particularly in Africa south of the Sahara. Since 2002 the situation has improved with an influx of additional resources for malaria control from the Global Fund to Fight AIDS, Tuberculosis, and Malaria. Over the last four rounds of country proposals, the Global Fund has stepped up its support by allocating about $450 million per year to malaria control and has created optimism and resolve among endemic countries to implement malaria control on a national scale. This is an encouraging start; however, more resources must be mobilized to meet the estimated need of $2–$3 billion per year for scaling up the response to malaria.

The Working Group on Malaria puts forward a global plan for scaling up country-level malaria control programs in endemic countries and makes a number of recommendations that require priority action to achieve the working group's proposed target for malaria: "Reduce malaria morbidity and mortality by 75 percent by 2015 from the 2005 baseline level." At the core of an operational framework is the implementation of integrated packages of effective antimalarial interventions designed to improve health nationally while also promoting economic development locally. Although this objective applies throughout the world's tropics, the need is particularly urgent in Sub-Saharan Africa.

A range of effective antimalarial tools and interventions exist for the prevention, treatment, and control of malaria

To this end, an integral part of this global plan is building stronger national health systems as a platform for delivering essential antimalarial commodities and effective interventions to those at risk of malaria. The public good will best be served by the free provision of insecticide-treated nets, application of residual insecticides, and provision of effective antimalarial medicines and diagnostics. Adequate information systems for health and effective management skills at national and district levels must complement provision of essential antimalarial commodities and services to ensure sustainability of disease control efforts. African countries, because of their marginalized position in the world economy and the scale of the malaria problem, are particularly vulnerable to any failure on the part of the international donor community to provide the necessary financial assistance.

A range of effective antimalarial tools and interventions exist for the prevention, treatment, and control of malaria. The components of a national malaria control strategy may include use of insecticide-treated nets; application of indoor residual spraying; early diagnosis of clinical infections; treatment with effective antimalarials; intermittent preventive treatment of pregnant women; management of the environment; improved housing; increased health education and awareness; epidemic forecasting, prevention, early detection, and control; and improved monitoring and surveillance systems and evaluation of program implementation. These interventions—if adapted to district- and village-level situations, implemented with sufficient intensity and coverage, and sustained on a national scale—will greatly reduce malaria morbidity and mortality and should promote economic growth. With adequate financial assistance, it is feasible to scale up access to interventions and increase low coverage levels to more than 80 percent in three to four years. Specifically, insecticide-treated bednets should be distributed to all children in malaria-endemic areas by 2007 to achieve 100 percent coverage. Such a comprehensive strategy would promote cognitive development and school attendance of young children. Finally, a program of applied and basic research is required to develop a series of alternative medicines and insecticides, rapid and reliable diagnostic tools suitable for field use, and appropriate vaccines.

The Working Group on Malaria has identified the following set of critical issues for priority action:

1. Establish a realistic and measurable target on malaria

Because the established Millennium Development Goal target on malaria, "Have halted by 2015 and begun to reverse the incidence of malaria" is difficult to measure and interpret, the Working Group on Malaria proposes a more measurable target. The revised target is recommended to be: "Reduce malaria morbidity and mortality by 75 percent by 2015 from the 2005 baseline level." The proposed target and timeline are consistent with the Millennium Development Goals for improved maternal health and reduction of child mortality, because children under five years of age and pregnant women are the most vulnerable to malaria.

Ministries of health need long-term predictable commitments of funding from the international donor community

2. Enhance commitment at country and global levels

Ministries of health should concentrate on their stewardship role by strengthening their planning, analytical, and public health expertise. Adequate human and financial resources should be dedicated to the pursuit of antimalarial interventions and the development of rationales for persuading other governmental agencies to join in this effort. Ministries such as agriculture, trade, mines, education, and finance are likely partners in malaria control. Such intersectoral collaborations are strengthened greatly when elements of the private sector such as philanthropic organizations and various industries (such as oil and mining) are included. Endemic countries should incorporate malaria control activities into their poverty reduction strategies.

Governments should promote the use of essential antimalarial intervention tools such as medicines, insecticides, insecticide-treated nets, and indoor residual spraying. Such public goods should be available free of cost to populations at risk for malaria. These efforts will require donor community participation to mobilize resources, as malaria-endemic countries cannot afford to implement these programs on their own. At the same time, measures should be adopted that will ensure the appropriate use of financial and other resources dedicated to malaria control interventions. Requirements for transparency should be imposed on agencies that are the recipients of such resources.

3. Strengthen health systems at national and district levels

Ministries of health need long-term predictable commitments of funding from the donor community to strengthen the healthcare infrastructure in endemic countries to provide quality laboratory services that will ensure reliable diagnosis and effective case management. Efficient mechanisms will also be required for procurement and distribution of medicines, reagents, insecticides, and other essential commodities, and for developing service delivery models coordinated with other health programs and effective health information and monitoring systems. These information systems would identify the most pressing health problems that can be addressed by existing technologies and also promote appropriate allocation of existing funds. Information systems for health should be modernized and strengthened and, as resources for health increase, should integrate community-level as well as facility-level data in a cohesive manner. Such comprehensive health information systems will enable planning, resource allocation, and tracking program performance through monitoring and evaluating process, outcome, and impact indicators. These systems are also essential for monitoring and evaluating program performance, assessing the equity of health systems, and evaluating the extent to which the Millennium Development Goals are realized.

4. Develop human resources for program implementation

Skilled personnel are required at national and district levels to assess local situations, develop appropriate intervention strategies, guide control activities

Essential antimalaria commodities should be provided free of charge to those at risk

and monitor their impact. Human resource constraints should be addressed through an appropriate combination of incentives, legislative measures, and management reforms. Motivated staff should be retained with salary supplements and hardship allowances, and housing should be provided for those working in rural areas where the malaria challenge is most pressing. Such incentives may also slow the exodus to other countries of professionals seeking better opportunities

Training is critically required in epidemiology, entomology, laboratory diagnostics, and case management. Materials and tools that would enhance supervision, planning, and program management should be developed and produced. Existing regional malaria training centers and networks should be encouraged to produce midlevel malaria professionals knowledgeable in malaria prevention and management. These midlevel professionals should also be able to implement malaria control activities effectively and promote advocacy and community participation. Current training programs, especially in Africa, lack mechanisms to track certificate holders. Monitoring and evaluation are keys to the enhancement of the quality of work at the community level.

5. Promote social mobilization and community participation

Systems should be put in place for mobilizing communities and encouraging community participation in malaria planning and control activities. Because a large majority of the population at risk in Sub-Saharan Africa lacks access to formal health services, extension health workers, traditional birth attendants, and community health agents have a central role in the prevention and treatment of malaria. Community participation in planning and implementing malaria control efforts should be supported as an integral part of an effective district health system. The process should include establishing new health centers and health posts as part of the district health system.

6. Provide effective antimalarial supplies and commodities

Antimalarial medicines, insecticide-treated nets, and insecticides for indoor residual spraying (mainly DDT and pyrethroids) should be considered public goods and should be available free of charge to residents of endemic sites.

7. Apply an integrated package of interventions

There is no single antimalarial "magic bullet" that can bring about a sustained reduction in the malaria burden. A combined set of locally adapted interventions should be used because the cycle of malaria transmission is composed of many components that vary greatly from place to place. This package of interventions includes use of insecticide-treated nets; the application of indoor residual spraying; early diagnosis of clinical infections; treatment with effective antimalarials; intermittent preventive treatment of pregnant women; management

Antimalarial intervention strategies should also promote social and economic development

of the environment; increased health education and awareness; epidemic forecasting, early detection and control; and improved monitoring and surveillance systems and evaluation of program implementation. The Working Group on Malaria endorses the Quick Wins initiative described in the UN Millennium Project's (2005) *Investing in Development*, which recommends immediate scale-up of high impact interventions that do not require complex infrastructure to implement. Among these Quick Wins is the recommendation that insecticide-treated bednets be distributed to all children in malaria-endemic areas by 2007. Because of the tremendous potential to save lives, especially in Sub-Saharan Africa, the working group believes that the target of 100 percent insecticide-treated bednet coverage among children should be an urgent international priority. In addition, intersectoral activities such as housing improvement, agricultural modification, water resource development, and road construction should complement these malaria-directed interventions.

8. Scale up malaria control efforts to national level
At present, malaria control efforts are conducted as relatively small projects with limited coverage and scope. Because they tend to be fragmented and unco-ordinated, these efforts have had little impact on the resurgence of malaria. Improving efficiency and use by expanding primary healthcare services and eliminating constraints and inadequacies are required. Control efforts should be intensified and coverage extended to include all malaria-endemic sites glob-ally. Community-based interventions should constitute an important element in the universal strategy. Ministries of health need major donor support to scale up investments in general health systems improvement and malaria con-trol to achieve the health-related Millennium Development Goals.

9. Promote social and economic development
Although the main objective is to reduce malaria-related mortality and mor-bidity, antimalarial intervention strategies should also promote social and eco-nomic development. Sustainability requires strategies designed to eliminate transmission in those sites that potentially generate wealth or that may promote social development. Wealth-generating sites include those that are devoted to tourism, mining, and manufacturing industries as well as port facilities. Social development is promoted in schools and administrative centers.

10. Incorporate malaria prevention and treatment approaches into school curricula
Instruction devoted to appropriate malaria-related material should be incor-porated into the curricula of health-related schools (those devoted to medi-cine, nursing, or sanitation) as well as schools devoted to agriculture, water resources, and civil engineering. Such material should also be included in pri-mary, secondary, and vocational schools.

Increased
development
assistance
is needed to
realize the
Millennium
Development
Goal target
for malaria

11. Develop surveillance systems for early detection of malaria epidemics

The increasing trend of large-scale malaria epidemics in the world requires the development of improved methods for epidemic forecasting, prevention, and early detection. Development of malaria surveillance systems is crucial for epidemic preparedness and effective response in epidemic-prone areas. Multisectoral approaches reinforce effective development of early warning systems and should be supported.

12. Promote partnerships for malaria control

Existing malaria partnerships link ministries of health with representatives of UN and donor agencies but provide limited opportunity for participation by other governmental sectors. Civil society, faith-based organizations, and the private sector are generally not included. Country-level partnerships should, therefore, include these nontraditional members, and the activities of these partner groups should be conducted under government ownership and leadership.

While some countries have set goals and targets in line with the health-related Millennium Development Goals, they are unlikely to achieve them on their own unless there is massive and sustained increase in development assistance from developed countries in order to help build national capacity for the successful large-scale implementation of programs in affected countries.

13. Secure affordable access to the latest medical and therapeutic discoveries

Development of sound policies to address the threat to health security due to the sharp increase in the prices of medicines and other commodities is required. To protect the poor nations from such a threat, such policies should envision a national patent regime to secure affordable access to the latest medical and therapeutic discoveries. Commitment is also required from the international community to alleviate the restrictive features of the Trade-Related Aspects of Intellectual Property Rights (TRIPS) agreement in its application to the health sector.

14. Invest in research and development on malaria control tools

Safe and affordable antimalarial medicines for case management, as well as other medicines suitable for prophylactic use or intermittent preventive treatment of pregnant women and their young children, are lacking. Because *P. falciparum* is increasingly losing its susceptibility to chloroquine and sulfadoxine-pyrimethamine (SP), such effective therapies as those based on artemisinin (that is, ACTs) or other novel effective antimalarials recommended by WHO should be made available for treating uncomplicated malaria. Strong financial support will be required for developing and testing new antimalarial medicines. Large-scale cultivation in Africa of the plant that is the source of artemisinin, *Artemisia annua* (annual wormwood), and a process for safely extracting and formulating the active ingredient should be supported and subsidized.

Development of new or improved diagnostic methods that are simple, reliable, and readily applicable in the field should be supported.

The availability of antimalarial vaccines is long overdue; vaccines suitable for use by long-term residents of endemic sites and others for use by transient residents are required.

Antivector methods effective against adult as well as larval mosquitoes should be improved, and new classes of insecticides developed.

Basic and operational research should be conducted for malaria epidemic forecasting, prevention, early detection, and rapid response.

Chapter 1

Introduction

The UN Millennium Project Task Force on HIV/AIDS, Malaria, TB, and Access to Essential Medicines aimed to devise a framework to accelerate the implementation of strategies for achieving Millennium Development Goal 6 to combat HIV/AIDS, malaria, and other diseases, with specific health improvements to be attained during the period 2005–15. Within this task force, the Working Group on Malaria has sought to develop an operational framework for relieving the burden that malaria imposes on society. Although this objective applies throughout the world's tropics, the need is particularly urgent in tropical Africa. The aim is to improve human well-being immediately while ultimately promoting economic growth.

Despite a series of declarations on malaria and pledges by global partners in the second half of the twentieth century, very few health gains have been translated into sustained societal improvements in the lives of those living in malaria-endemic areas, particularly in tropical Africa where malaria transmission has historically been far more intense than elsewhere. Success stories, notably during the Global Malaria Eradication Campaign (1955–69), have been confined largely to areas of low malaria transmission, mainly in the temperate and subtropical regions of the world.

A curtailment of commitment and resources for malaria control and research characterizes the decades following the global eradication period, as malaria has become a disease of the poor nations located primarily in tropical areas. National malaria control programs have been fragmented, lacking in organizational structure and human and economic resources needed for sustainable implementation. The malaria problem has been compounded by the development and spread of resistance to effective and affordable antimalarial medicines and insecticides, especially since the 1980s. The growing HIV/AIDS

> **The public good will best be served if essential antimalarial commodities and services are provided free of charge in developing countries**

pandemic has also overstretched the already-limited resources available for disease control in the past decade, particularly in Africa.

Launched in 1998 by the World Health Organization (WHO), Roll Back Malaria has successfully harnessed the necessary political commitment for malaria control within the international donor community.[2] The level of internal commitment from African countries rose sharply following the Abuja Summit on Malaria held in April 2000. At present, a broad consensus exists for a coordinated effort aiming to strengthen systems for delivering effective malaria control interventions on a sustainable basis. Country-level implementation of the Roll Back Malaria initiative has been severely limited, however, because of donors' reluctance to commit resources for large-scale procurement of essential health commodities such as antimalarial medicines, mosquito nets, and insecticides. Consequently, resource-poor malaria-endemic countries have been unable to undertake nationwide control activities, resorting instead, to programs of limited scope. Since 2002, the situation has improved with an influx of additional resources for malaria control from the Global Fund to Fight AIDS, Tuberculosis, and Malaria (GFATM), which resulted in several country-led initiatives with well defined objectives, targets, and indicators.

The public good will best be served if essential antimalarial commodities are provided free of charge in developing countries, especially Sub-Saharan Africa. Particularly important is distributing insecticide-treated bednets, applying residual insecticides, and providing effective antimalarial medicine and diagnostics to those at risk for malaria at no cost (Bradley 2001; Curtis and others 2003; Curtis 2002b). Adequate information systems for health and effective management skills, applied at national and district levels, must complement the provision of essential commodities and services. Human resource development is another area that is emerging as an urgent priority for sustainable disease control efforts.

The Millennium Development Goal and target for malaria

As enunciated in the UN Millennium Declaration, the UN Millennium Project has the following time-bound target for malaria: "Have halted by 2015 and begun to reverse the incidence of malaria." Because this target is difficult to interpret and measure, the Working Group on Malaria proposes a more measurable target: "Reduce malaria morbidity and mortality by 75 percent by 2015 from the 2005 baseline level." The proposed target and timeline are consistent with the overall health objective and with the Millennium Development Goals and targets that focus on improving the health of pregnant women and young children, those who are most vulnerable to malaria.

Sustainability will be gained by an accompanying objective that focuses on economic advancement, seeking to create malaria-free zones in which trade, industry, and tourism will flourish.

Success in overcoming challenges to implementation should enable many countries to develop and maintain effective malaria control programs

To ensure this level of impact, the following coverage targets for key interventions should be achieved by the year 2008:

- Eighty percent of people at risk for malaria are protected by a suitable combination of locally appropriate vector control interventions (insecticide-treated bednets, indoor residual spraying, and environmental management).
- Eighty percent of malaria patients are diagnosed by means of rapid, sensitive, and specific tests and treated with effective antimalarial medicines, such as artemisinin-based combination therapies (ACTs), within one day of the onset of illness.

Organization of this report

This document is organized into 10 chapters. After an overview of the health and socioeconomic burden and the resurgence of the disease, it presents a summary of major initiatives and institutional policies that have been undertaken for malaria control. Key malaria control strategies are described and several successful scaling-up experiences are reviewed. The document then discusses major challenges to implementing malaria control programs designed to reduce the burden that malaria imposes on society and describes circumstances that obstruct the attainment of necessary resources.

The Working Group on Malaria puts forward key strategies for effective scaling up of integrated packages of locally relevant malaria control interventions in endemic countries and makes a number of recommendations that require priority action. Success in overcoming challenges to implementation should enable many countries to develop and maintain effective malaria control programs and thereby achieve the Millennium Development Goal and target for malaria by the year 2015.

This document is intended for governments of malaria-endemic countries, partner institutions in developed countries, private sector agencies, nongovernmental foundations, civil society organizations, nongovernmental organizations (NGOs), and academic and research institutes. The recommendations herein are also outlined in the UN Millennium Project's (2005) *Investing in Development: A Practical Plan to Achieve the Millennium Development Goals.*

An analysis of the global cost of scaling up a set of antimalarial interventions was commissioned by WHO in support of the UN Millennium Project's Working Group on Malaria. The global cost for 2005–15 is estimated to be $31.9 billion, which corresponds to about $3 billion per year.[3] Costing details and assumptions are presented in chapter 7.

The results of a preliminary needs assessment for nationwide scaled-up malaria control in Ethiopia between 2005 and 2015 are presented in appendix 1. This needs assessment indicates that the total cost of an integrated package of interventions for the next 10 years is estimated to be about $2.6 billion in Ethiopia. Although the initial cost of the intervention package is estimated to be large, intervention costs should decrease progressively because the capital costs and number of malaria cases will decrease over time. The annual per capita costs are estimated to decrease from $6.20 to $2.40 between 2005 and 2010 and from $2.40 to $0.84 between 2010 and 2015.

Chapter 2

The resurgence and burden of malaria

Despite a century of systematic disease control efforts, malaria is still rampant in several regions of the world (map 2.1), draining the vitality of about 100 nations, particularly in Africa south of the Sahara (WHO 2002). More than 50 percent of the world's population is at risk of malaria infection today. During the Global Malaria Eradication Campaign between 1955 and 1969, malaria disappeared from the former Soviet Union, southern Europe, the United States, all but one of the Caribbean islands, and Taiwan (China). It was effectively suppressed in several subtropical and tropical regions in southern Africa, Latin America, parts of Asia, and the Middle East. Tropical Africa was, however, excluded from the eradication campaign, and it and New Guinea are the only regions in which the malaria burden persisted at high intensity throughout the twentieth century.

In the past three decades, malaria has, however, encroached upon areas where it had formerly been eradicated or had successfully been controlled (Baird 2000), offsetting the gains attained in the latter half of the past century. Increasing parasite resistance to commonly used antimalarial medicines is one of the most significant challenges facing malaria control efforts in most endemic countries (Teklehaimanot 1986; Wolfe and others 1985). Chloroquine resistance is widespread where *falciparum* malaria is endemic, except in Central America and the Caribbean (Wongsrichanalai and others 2002). Sulfadoxine-pyrimethamine (SP) resistance has been reported in large parts of Southeast Asia, southern China, the Amazon basin, western Oceania, the Pacific coast, and parts of Africa (Guerin and others 2002; Sibley and others 2001). The increasing risk of severe disease and death due to resistance threatens primarily the high-risk populations in malaria-stricken areas, particularly young children (Trape and others 1998).[1] Parasite resistance to commonly used antimalarial medicines has been suggested to be the main cause of marked increases in

Map 2.1

Malaria remains firmly entrenched in tropical developing countries, 2004

Source: World Health Organization, Roll Back Malaria Department.

High malaria transmission   Low malaria transmission   Malaria-free

Young children and pregnant women bear the brunt of the malaria burden in endemic areas

malaria mortality rates in eastern and southern Africa from 1982 to 1989 and from 1990 to 1998 (Korenromp and others 2003).

The epidemiologic variability of malaria has important consequences for public health in general, and for malaria control efforts in particular. Environmental changes, socioeconomic factors, and political circumstances have led to a complex distribution of the disease across the globe, rendering malaria's containment intractable within the limits of currently available financial and technical resources.

Health burden

Assessment of the true scale of the disease burden is fraught with formidable challenges due to insufficient surveillance, underreporting, and problems in attributing "a cause" of death in people who die at home without reaching a health facility and often suffer from diarrhea and respiratory disease as well as fever. Malaria, however, is estimated to cause 300–500 million episodes of acute illness and 1.1–2.7 million deaths worldwide every year (WHO 2000c). Tropical Africa, where the disease transmission is most favored by a set of epidemiological, ecological, and socioeconomic factors, carries more than 90 percent of the global malaria burden. In Africa, resistance to chloroquine by *P. falciparum* was first detected in Tanzania (Campbell and others 1979) and spread rapidly to eastern, central, and southern parts of the continent (Nguyen-Dinh 1985; Teklehaimanot 1986; Wolfe and others 1985). With an increasing level of multimedicine resistance, the Indian subcontinent and Southeast Asia bear most of the remaining burden (WHO 2004d) (map 2.2). Released in December 2003, the *African Malaria Report* indicated that "current malaria control efforts are acting against a background of increasing malaria burden" (WHO and UNICEF 2003).

Lacking acquired immunity to the disease, young children bear the brunt of malaria mortality, which accounts for at least 20 percent of overall childhood deaths in Africa south of the Sahara (WHO and UNICEF, 2003). Without effective interventions, the number of febrile episodes in children under five years of age is estimated to double over the next two decades (Breman 2001). Poor nutritional status as a risk factor has been associated with increased malaria morbidity and mortality, particularly in young children (Shankar 2000). Besides children, pregnant women with suppressed immune systems, particularly those in their first pregnancy in highly endemic areas, are at great risk of acute malaria infections with a range of clinical outcomes, from anemia to severe complications such as cerebral malaria (Menendez 1995). Malaria infection during pregnancy exacts a toll on the infants as well, as it has been associated with low birthweight, affecting the survival and development of newborns, especially in Africa (Murphy and Breman 2001).

Several studies have shown that people living in poorly constructed houses in endemic areas experience more vector contact and are at greater risk of

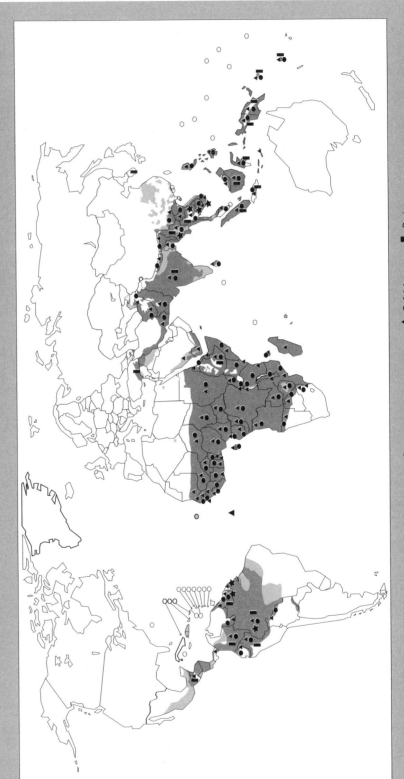

Map 2.2
Resistance to commonly used antimalarials is widespread, 2004

Source: World Health Organization, Roll Back Malaria Department.

High malaria transmission

Low malaria transmission

Malaria-free

▲ *P. falciparum* chloroquine resistance

● *P. falciparum* sulfadoxine-pyrimethamine resistance

★ *P. falciparum* mefloquine failure

■ *P. vivax* chloroquine failure

Inhabitants of poorly built houses are most likely to suffer from malaria

malaria infection than those living in well constructed houses (Gamage-Mendis and others 1991; Gunawardena and others 1998; Konradsen and others 2003; Lindsay and others 2003). Overall, the quality of housing is connected mainly with socioeconomic status of households. Therefore, once infected, inhabitants of poorly built houses are most likely to suffer from malaria because of their limited capacity to use preventive and treatment services and commodities. In rural Tanzania, mortality in children less than five years old following acute fever was reported to be 39 percent higher among the poorest as opposed to the least poor (Barat and others 2004). People living in remote and poverty-stricken rural areas in tropical Asia and the Americas need to migrate frequently to sustain their livelihood, exposing them to malaria, yet they have limited access to healthcare services (Singhanetra-Renard 1986). Lack of basic education leads to inadequate healthcare-seeking (Sharma and others 1993). Distance from health services and opportunity costs of lost work time are also potentially important nonfinancial factors for serious malaria complications in the poor (Barat and others 2004).

Today, malaria is a major public health problem in urban settings, where it is estimated to cause 3–9 million cases every year (WHO 2001b). Rapid and unplanned urban growth in tropical areas creates suitable conditions for malaria transmission, mainly at the periphery of towns and cities. People who migrate from rural areas generally settle in poorly constructed houses in densely populated and underdeveloped periurban areas and bring along their traditional rural practices (such as farming in small garden plots with small-scale irrigation) that favor mosquito breeding. In India, one of the main vectors, *A. stephensi,* has become highly adapted to artificial breeding places found in urban environments over the last decades, leading to increased urban malaria problem (Sharma 1999). Entomological surveys carried out in Kenya found that recent land use changes and, in particular, recent urbanization and construction activities were positively associated with anopheline breeding activity (Jacob and others 2003; Khaemba, Mutani, and Bett 1994).

Engineering and development projects such as the construction of dams, roads, and industrial centers may increase the number of mosquito breeding habitats and lead to disease propagation in malaria-prone areas (Patz and others 2000). On the other hand, human interference may sometimes reduce malaria transmission by making ecological niches unsuitable for local vectors. For instance, organic pollution of most surface water in urbanized areas makes it unsuitable for *Anopheles* larvae but highly suitable for *Culex* mosquitoes, and deforestation in Thailand led to the cessation of malaria transmission in certain regions (Oaks and others 1991).

Another concern is the incursion of nonimmune people into forests and jungles for agriculture, road construction, timbering, and gem mining where malaria vectors are abundant (Nájera, Liese, and Hammer 1992). For instance, the Amazon Basin Settlement Project drew nonimmune people into

**In the
decades
following
the global
eradication
period,
political
commitment
and resources
for malaria
control have
dwindled**

the region for mining activities, resulting in a proliferation of the malaria vector in artificial habitats and consequent malaria epidemics (Marques 1987; Molyneux 1998). In Africa, major resettlement programs that involve the movement of largely nonimmune highland populations into high-transmission lowland areas constitute a major problem. In Ethiopia, for example, resettlement programs in the Gambella region have been associated with a dramatic rise in malaria incidence over the past 15 years. The deleterious effects of large population movements on malaria incidence are often exacerbated by land-use changes associated with resettlement itself (Nigatu, Abebe and Dejene 1992; Woube 1997).

Summary of temporal trends in the malaria burden

Historically, malaria plagued tropical and temperate regions of the world. Until the mid-nineteenth century, malaria occurred as far north as Maine and Vermont in the United States, even spilling over to Canada. Disappearance of the disease from vast regions in North America and central Europe has been primarily attributed to land reclamation efforts for agriculture, increased animal husbandry, improvements in housing, and the other effects of economic development (Bruce-Chwatt 1988).

In the beginning of the twentieth century, malaria was a major health problem in southern Europe, Latin America, the western Pacific, the Caribbean, much of Asia, and the Middle East. The global malaria picture was altered considerably during the Global Eradication Campaign between 1955 and 1969. With the exception of the former Soviet Union, southern Europe, North America, and some islands, the goal of malaria eradication set forth in the last century was never realized (Litsios 1996). However, unprecedented reductions in the prevalence of malaria were achieved in northern and southern Africa, the Middle East, South and East Asia, and Latin America (Roberts, Manguin, and Mouchet 2000). Despite the vast scale of the malaria problem on the African continent, tropical African countries were only partially involved in the global eradication program (Greenwood and Mutabingwa 2002).

In the decades following the global eradication period, political commitment and resources allocated for malaria control and research have dwindled and malaria has become a disease of the poor nations situated mainly in tropical areas (Shiffman, Beer, and Wu 2002). Moreover, during the 1970s and 1980s, national health systems underwent substantial reforms in many developing countries, moving from a strategy based on vertically organized disease-specific programs to one based on the delivery of integrated health services. "Primary health care" was adopted as a key concept around which health systems were organized (Mayhew 1996). In many countries, these developments resulted in a series of decentralized healthcare systems that diluted the force of disease-specific programs in most countries.

Other important challenges to malaria control come from population movements associated with economic development and civil conflicts

Main factors affecting malaria trends

Despite the general degradation of malaria control programs during the 1990s, a number of endemic countries outside of Africa have made notable progress in malaria control (for example, China, Thailand, Vanuatu, and Viet Nam; Sharma 2002). However, rising rates of multimedicine resistance in *P. falciparum* and the emergence of chloroquine resistance in *P. vivax* are posing formidable challenges for malaria control efforts in Asia, especially in the southeastern parts of the continent (Pukrittayakamee and others 2004). The Mekong region has been identified as the global epicenter of multimedicine resistant malaria (Schapira 2002). ASIA - lots of resistance

Other important challenges to malaria control come from population movements associated with economic development and civil conflicts. The gold and gem mining and logging in South America (as in the Amazon basin) and Southeast Asia (as in Myanmar, Thailand, and Sri Lanka) have been important in intensifying malaria transmission in forested areas by exposing nonimmune populations to the pathogen (Sharma 2002). In a number of countries (such as Afghanistan, Ethiopia, the Democratic Republic of Congo, Sudan, and Tajikistan), the malaria situation has become exacerbated due to social and political instabilities deriving from large-scale population movements and inadequate health services.

Lack of adequate health delivery systems to effectively deliver antimalarial medicines and other interventions and human and technical resource constraints lie at the heart of the malaria problem (Teklehaimanot and Bosman 1999). Because of their marginalized position in the world economy and the extent of the malaria problem, African countries are particularly vulnerable to any failure on part of the international donor community to supply effective antimalarials and other essential supplies and commodities for malaria control.

lot (a failure on donor comm

Economic and social burden

The disease burden imposed by malaria carries with it a corresponding economic burden. Several studies have been undertaken to estimate the economic impact of malaria by focusing on direct prevention and treatment costs borne by households and the public health sector. Some studies have also considered income losses due to malaria morbidity as indirect costs of the disease. In rural communities, especially in Africa, the economy is heavily dependent on agriculture, and the malaria transmission season generally coincides with that of planting or harvesting, leading to reduced agricultural productivity and output (Girardin and others 2004). Anecdotal evidence suggests that families living in disease-stricken areas, including those with a high burden of malaria, favor less labor-demanding crops over higher value crops such as maize and rice (Hoek 2004). Many subsistence farmers in Africa shoulder the heaviest burden of malaria because their margin of survival is so fragile. A brief period of illness that delays planting or coincides with the harvest may produce catastrophic

Malaria endemicity has recently been recognized as a development issue with a key influence on poverty reduction

economic effects. This problem becomes exacerbated when antimalarial medicines and insecticide-treated bednets must be purchased out of the farming household's meager cash reserves (Ettling and others 1994). A recent study found that 58 percent of the malaria cases occurred in the poorest 20 percent of the world's population (Gwatkin and Guillot 1999). Investments in malaria control should aim at improving the quality of life in the poorest populations who coexist with this disease.

Malaria endemicity has recently been recognized as a development issue with a key influence on poverty reduction. This infection has been estimated to slow economic growth in African countries by about 1.3 percent per year (Gallup and Sachs 2001). This disease incapacitates the workforce, leading to decreased economic productivity and output in various sectors of the economy (Shepard and others 1991; Sinton 1936, 1935). Malaria suppresses economic links between tropical countries and the more temperate regions of the world that are generally nonmalarious (Sachs and Malaney 2002).

In today's global economy, such isolation carries profoundly negative effects. Investors from nonmalarious regions tend to shun malarious regions for fear that their employees will contract this disease. Mortality among highly skilled professionals strongly discourages economic investment in malaria-endemic sites. Investments in many kinds of production—in mining, agriculture, and manufacturing—can be crippled if the labor force faces a heavy disease burden, or if the presence of malaria raises the cost of attracting needed labor. During the colonial period between 1900 and 1950, malaria control was frequently decisive in attracting the labor force that was essential for extracting minerals in Zambia (formerly Northern Rhodesia) (Utzinger and others 2002; Utzinger, Tozan, and Singer 2001) and for developing rubber and tea plantations in Malaysia (formerly the Malay States) (Watson 1921). Rubber plantations in Southeast Asia still depend on effective malaria control. During the past several decades, international trade and finance have become critical for economic development. Malaria-induced adverse effects on trade and investment are likely to be of tremendous macroeconomic importance, slowing economic growth and further widening the gap between malaria-endemic countries and the rest of the world.

In 2004, the Copenhagen Consensus expert panel, comprising top-level economists, ranked malaria control among the four greatest global challenges, along with control of HIV/AIDS, providing micronutrients, and trade liberalization (Copenhagen Consensus 2004). Based on macroeconomic models, the analysis presented to the expert panel estimated that the annualized net benefits of reducing the malaria burden by 50 percent between 2002 and 2015 would be between $3 billion and $10 billion with a benefit-cost ratio ranging from 1.9 to 4.7 (Mills and Shillcutt 2004a, 2004b). Based on the available cost-effectiveness data from tropical Africa, the total annualized cost of a package of malaria interventions (including scaling up of insecticide-treated bednets and treatment coverage, introducing intermittent preventive treatment with SP in pregnancy, and switching first-line treatment to ACTs for 346 million people, was estimated at $824 million (Mills and Shillcutt 2004b).

Chapter 3

Review of major initiatives and institutional policies for malaria control

Over the past 50 years, the major concepts and strategies underlying global malaria control efforts have undergone a series of changes. The principal initiatives and institutional policies of malaria control in the modern era are summarized below and provide the framework within which the main recommendations of the Working Group on Malaria were developed.

Global Malaria Eradication Program

Intractability?

The availability of dichlorodiphenyltrichloroethane (DDT) and the profound effect of indoor residual spraying on malaria transmission encouraged the world to attempt to eradicate the disease globally. The Global Malaria Eradication Program began during the 1950s and ended in the following decade. Due to the perceived intractability of malaria in tropical Africa and concern of sustainability, the Global Program largely bypassed this continent where the malaria burden was greatest. During the next several decades, the malaria problem, particularly in Africa, attracted little interest. Scant resources were allocated by the international donor community to disease control efforts leading to poorly coordinated and fragmented intervention programs in malarious areas.

Global Malaria Control Strategy

Malaria has been a subject of intense discussion at the annual meetings of the World Health Assembly over the last decade. The 1990 meeting of the Assembly attributed the global resurgence of malaria to rapidly increasing antimalarial medicine resistance, the lack of a clear control strategy, and an acute shortage of financial resources. The Assembly recommended that an appropriate disease control strategy be developed and that a coordinated effort for mobilizing resources be undertaken to intensify disease control efforts. The Amsterdam

Malaria has been a subject of intense discussion at the annual meetings of the World Health Assembly over the last decade

Ministerial Conference on Malaria of 1992 adopted a global malaria control strategy that was endorsed by the UN General Assembly in 1993. The four basic technical elements of the Global Malaria Control Strategy were as follows (WHO 1993):

- Provision of early diagnosis and prompt treatment.
- Selective and sustainable use of preventive measures, including vector control.
- Prevention, early detection, and containment of epidemics.
- Strengthening local capacities in basic and applied research.

This strategy recognized that the epidemiology of malaria is exceedingly complex and that local variation in the ecological, social, and operational aspects of the disease should be considered for developing appropriate strategies. This strategy was well received by the international community and malaria-endemic countries, and great expectations were generated for meaningful engagement in malaria control efforts. Despite this initial enthusiasm, the donor community failed to mobilize the resources necessary for undertaking nationwide control efforts.

Harare Declaration on Malaria Prevention and Control

At a Summit meeting in 1997, the heads of state of the Organization of African Unity took particular note of the deteriorating malaria situation in Africa and unanimously passed a Declaration on Malaria Prevention and Control that was designed to promote African economic recovery and development. The Summit approved a comprehensive intervention plan for malaria and called upon all member states to take immediate and substantive action. UN agencies, the World Bank, various governments, and bilateral and multilateral agencies were urged to participate actively in the effort and mobilize additional resources to meet the challenge of malaria on the African continent. This potentially powerful commitment has also faltered due to lack of international support.

Multilateral Initiative on Malaria

In 1997, key scientific and donor agencies convened in Dakar, Senegal, to discuss collaborative efforts to address pressing health problems in Africa. Malaria was selected as the initial focus of this effort. Subsequently, the Multilateral Initiative on Malaria (MIM) was created with the aim of maximizing the impact of scientific research on malaria in Africa. The primary goal of MIM is to address several important areas of need in malaria control (MIM 2001). First, it was recognized that the investment in malaria research was low relative to the burden of disease and that existing control tools were not being effectively utilized. Second, malaria was recognized as a problem that required short-, medium- and long-term research priorities in order to be contained effectively. Third, in view of the existing inequality between knowledge of the disease—its pathology and etiology—and its reduction in endemic countries,

The Roll Back Malaria initiative achieved notable consensus among its partners on malaria control

MIM highlighted the importance of strengthening research capacity in Africa This aim was to be accomplished through collaboration and communication between scientists in Europe and United States and those in the endemic countries of Africa. The combination of these efforts has culminated in several effective partnerships between scientists from developed countries and their African counterparts.

Roll Back Malaria initiative

The Roll Back Malaria (RBM) initiative was conceived by WHO in 1998 in response to a call by ministers of health in malaria-endemic countries to reduce the malaria burden worldwide, with a special focus on Africa (WHO 1998). Subsequently, the global RBM partnership was formed under the auspices of the WHO, comprising the United Nations Development Programme the United Nations Children's Fund, and the World Bank, with the specific goal of halving the burden of malaria by 2010. RBM adopted the malaria control strategies that were accepted by the international community in the Amsterdam Ministerial Conference of 1992, focusing on principles of coordinated action and partnership.

The RBM initiative has achieved notable consensus among its partners on malaria control. It has been instrumental in developing and formulating country-led partnerships that include UN agencies, bilateral donors, various government sectors, civil society organizations, NGOs, the private sector, universities, and research institutions. A number of malaria-endemic countries have put together evidence-based strategic plans for implementation that are based on an analysis of their local ecological and epidemiological conditions in order to address the burden of the disease within the context of health sector development. Despite the recognition and acceptance of the RBM goals, targets, and strategy, the RBM initiative—apart from the initial grant it received from the government of the United Kingdom—has been unable to mobilize resources to launch countrywide implementation efforts (WHO 2002) and has made no impact on the malaria problem, particularly in Africa.

Abuja Declaration on Roll Back Malaria

The African Summit on the Roll Back Malaria initiative, held in Abuja Nigeria, in April 2000, reflected a strong convergence of political commitment to malaria control and a consensus on the technical strategies for the prevention and control of malaria. The heightened level of political will was facilitated by the presence of high-level officials from African countries as well as various bilateral and multilateral agencies, and resulted in the ratification of an action-oriented declaration. The African Summit endorsed the RBM initiative and set operational targets and milestones for the RBM objectives. A commitment was given to provide access to effective and affordable treatment within eight hours of the onset of symptoms for at least 60 percent of those

Many African governments have demonstrated their commitment to antimalarial intervention efforts

suffering from malaria. In the area of prevention, a target was set to achieve at least 60 percent coverage of those at risk of malaria, particularly pregnant women and children, with personal and community protective measures such as insecticide-treated nets. Another preventive target set forth was to provide access to intermittent presumptive treatment for at least 60 percent of pregnant women who are at risk of malaria. In high-transmission areas, this target focuses on women who are in their first pregnancies, as they are at great risk of developing severe malaria.

Many of the major international donors that participated in the Summit, including the World Bank and the African Development Bank, pledged increased commitment and resources. The World Bank alone committed $500 million for controlling malaria (Yamey 2001). However, this pledge was not translated into action as the indicated grant funds were not provided to either RBM or endemic countries.

Since the Abuja summit, many African governments have demonstrated their commitment to antimalarial intervention efforts by allocating greater human and financial resources and removing taxes and tariffs on mosquito nets. No pledges, however, have yet materialized that would enable RBM to support endemic countries in implementing an integrated package of interventions on national scales.

Medicines for Malaria Venture

Headquartered in Geneva, the Medicines for Malaria Venture (MMV) was established as a nonprofit foundation in 1999. It developed in response to discussions between WHO (primarily through WHO's Special Program on Research and Training for Tropical Diseases), RBM, the representative body for the pharmaceutical industry, and the International Federation of Pharmaceutical Manufacturers Association. MMV uses the public-private partnership model, with funding from philanthropic organizations, to facilitate discovery, development, and delivery of new, affordable antimalarial medicines. Direct financial support to the MMV was provided by the World Bank, RBM, and others, while various corporate partners directed in-kind contributions for specific projects. Since its inception, the MMV has played a significant role in streamlining research aimed at finding new antimalarial medicines by providing managerial and logistical support through active portfolio management. MMV's primary goal is to increase the success rate of potential antimalarial therapies on an average of discovery and development of one medicine every five years. As of June 2004, the MMV has a total of 21 projects, 11 in the discovery phase and 10 in the development phase (MMV 2004).

Global Fund to fight AIDS, Tuberculosis, and Malaria

The Global Fund to fight AIDS, Tuberculosis, and Malaria (GFATM) was created by UN Secretary-General Kofi Annan to support national efforts aimed at

**It is critical
that the
international
donor
community
provide
financial
support to
strengthen
the GFATM**

reducing the burden of HIV/AIDS, tuberculosis, and malaria. Each of the G-8 countries has committed itself to support this action. The GFATM funding process requires formal submission of a proposal by malaria-endemic countries and evaluation by a review panel that includes members who are expert in one or another of these diseases. Although this concept has received general support, criticism has been directed toward the mechanisms for reviewing country proposals and the selection of panel members. Each panel member should have experience in implementing and managing malaria control programs and should be given adequate time to review each country's proposal (Teklehaimanot and Snow 2002). No panel member, of course, should have conflict of interest.

With an approved budget of $3 billion for all three diseases over two years, the GFATM has allocated and started disbursing a total of $921 million at the end of four proposal rounds for 80 malaria-endemic countries (GFATM 2004a). The HIV/AIDS and tuberculosis allocations amount to $1.8 billion in 119 countries and $500 million in 80 countries respectively.

Although the GFATM provides a much-needed complement to existing public health funding, its available funding budget is not sufficient for countries to launch comprehensive intervention packages at the national scale. Nevertheless, the GFATM has taken a more proactive role in facilitating a more rapid transition to safe and effective antimalarial therapies, such as ACTs, where resistance to existing medicines is a problem, and has committed to providing funding for procuring and distributing these antimalarials (GFATM 2004b). The input of the GFATM has thus made a significant difference by motivating a number of malaria-endemic countries to update their national antimalaria treatment policies and to scale up existing malaria control interventions. It critical that the international donor community provide financial support to strengthen the GFATM and its funded initiatives.

Chapter 4

Malaria control strategies

A variety of integrated packages of locally relevant interventions can, in principle, be implemented against malaria using available tools. The components of such intervention strategies include:

- Disease prevention.
- Disease management.
- Epidemic prevention and control.
- Information, education, and communication.
- Monitoring and evaluation.

The selection and implementation of interventions, as well as the nature of program monitoring and evaluation depend to a large extent on the country, the district, and the community in which the program is based. The essential features of currently available malaria control interventions are reviewed below.

Disease prevention strategies

The force of malaria transmission can most effectively be reduced by curtailing the capacity of local mosquito vectors to transmit infection between human hosts (Spielman, Kitron, and Pollack 1993). There is an array of effective interventions that can affect important vector-related factors—such as vector abundance, biting density, and vector longevity—that drive disease proliferation. Interventions that are based on the use of insecticides will be less sustainable than those that involve environmental change or housing modification. Key disease-prevention measures that target the malaria vector are discussed below.

Insecticide-treated materials

Bednets, curtains, and other insecticide-treated materials provide both a chemical and a physical barrier against malaria vector mosquitoes. These measures are effective in Africa because the major vector mosquitoes bite late at night.

Long-lasting insecticidal nets can provide several years of protection

When there is a high level of coverage within a community, insecticide-treated bednets protect the individuals sleeping under them and also reduce local vector populations and proportions carrying the malaria parasite by reducing mosquito longevity (Magesa and others 1991; Takken 2002). Both effects are crucial and can most rapidly and economically be achieved if insecticide-treated bednets are provided free of charge to all members of a community, along with a well organized annual retreatment program (Curtis and others 2003). The reductions achieved in malaria prevalence, anemia, and mortality are estimated to persist for at least 3 to 6 years (Lindblade and others 2004; Maxwell and others 2002). The use of insecticide-treated bednets has resulted in an average of six lives saved per year per 1,000 children and is highly effective in both high- and low-transmission settings (Lengeler 1998; Maxwell and others 2003).

Long-lasting insecticidal nets, which are made from polyethylene fiber into which insecticide is embedded, may be used in place of insecticide-treated bednets to eliminate the need for annual retreatment (N'Guessan and others 2003). Long-lasting insecticidal nets provide several years of protection before retreatment becomes necessary (WHO 2003c). They are physically more durable than ordinary insecticide-treated bednets, which must be replaced every four years.

Indoor residual spraying

Applications of residual insecticide, especially DDT, to the inside surfaces of house walls and on ceilings was the main method used to eliminate malaria from southern Europe, the highlands of Madagascar, most of the former Soviet Union, and Taiwan (China) in the 1940s and 1950s (Litsios 1996). DDT application was also the primary activity of the massive antimalaria efforts undertaken in the 1950s and 1960s in China, India, South Africa, Sri Lanka, Zanzibar, in some parts of South America, and in several large field trials in mainland tropical Africa (Gladwell 2002; Liang 1991; Litsios 1996; Trigg and Kondrachine, 1998). The resumption of DDT spraying led to the resolution of the disastrous Madagascan epidemic of the 1980s that killed tens of thousands of people (Curtis 2002a). Many of these trials or operations produced better results than more recent trials that have employed insecticide-treated bednets (Curtis and Mnzava 2000). In Zanzibar and in some parts of western Africa, DDT resistance in *A. gambiae* now precludes the effective use of this insecticide. The chemical is still being used in large scale in Ethiopia, India, Madagascar, and South Africa. The decision by South Africa to revert to DDT spraying in 2001 has relieved the increasing malaria problem associated with pyrethroid resistance in *A. funestus* (Hargreaves and others 2000).

The International Convention on Persistent Organic Pollutants contains an amendment that specifically allows for continued use of DDT for disease vector control (UNEP 2004). There are effective but more expensive

There are effective but more expensive alternative insecticides to DDT

alternatives to DDT (such as pyrethroids) that can be sprayed where the local vector populations are DDT resistant and are at the same time not cross-resistant to the alternative insecticide. The use of carbamates in a rural and a peri-urban spraying program has successfully reduced the number of malaria cases in southern Mozambique during the first implementation year (Conteh and others 2004). The use of indoor residual spraying against malaria is particularly recommended in epidemic-prone areas and complex emergency settings and, more generally, in low- and moderate-transmission areas. Availability of well trained and properly equipped spray-men for deployment is critical to the effective implementation of indoor residual spraying during malaria epidemics.

Antilarval measures for source reduction

Because the breeding places of *A. gambiae* are numerous and transient in many African villages, they are often difficult to eliminate. In towns, semi-arid regions, and mining areas where breeding sites are few and the necessary workforce can be mobilized, vector density and malaria prevalence may be reduced through the implementation of antilarval measures. In Sri Lanka, the application of an insect growth regulator to gem pits effectively reduced adult vector populations, prevalence of infection, and case incidence (Yapabandara and others 2001).

Large-scale rural-to-urban migration in many African cities has been accompanied by a substantial and ongoing transformation of local ecosystems. The process of urbanization simultaneously leads to source reduction or shifts in the location and character of breeding sites within the changing boundaries of the inner city. As city boundaries expand, breeding sites tend to proliferate peripherally, particularly in new settlement areas. At the same time, human activities associated with the creation of breeding sites, such as urban agriculture, may change in intensity and location as the city grows. For effective control, specialized strategies including risk mapping must be integrated into malaria control programs in urban areas. An example of a successful and innovative approach to urban malaria control comes from Dar-es-Salaam, where risk mapping of malaria breeding sites and the identification of locally relevant source reduction techniques provided the basis for developing more effective control strategies (Castro and others 2004).

Many malaria-endemic urban centers in Africa are surrounded by malarious rural villages—a setting that renders it difficult to distinguish locally contracted infections from those occurring in people who come to these urban centers for treatment. Because the epidemiological factors shaping malaria transmission in urban environments are not well understood, WHO has recently commissioned a multicenter study of urban malaria transmission. Where appropriate, source reduction measures may reasonably be employed in urban areas to suppress transmission.

Maternal malaria has important consequences for the mother, the developing fetus, and the infant

Source reduction by intermittent irrigation strategies has been effectively used since the 1920s to control rice field malaria, primarily in Asia (Lu 1988 Takken and others 1990). In a number of instances, these irrigation scheme: have reduced the vector populations and also changed nutrient cycling pat terns, increasing rice production to levels above that attained by conventiona irrigation (that is, continuous flooding) (Keiser and others 2002). The oppor tunity to expand the domain of intermittent irrigation together with the devel opment of new high-yield strains of rice is gradually being taken up by the International Rice Research Institute (IRRI) and linked to malaria control via the Systemwide Initiative on Malaria and Agriculture (SIMA) and the Inter national Water Management Institute (IWMI).

Malaria management in pregnancy

More than 50 million pregnancies—approximately 25 million of them in Africa—are estimated to occur in malaria-affected areas every year (Steketee and others 2001). Maternal malaria has important consequences for th mother, the developing fetus, and the infant. In high-transmission areas maternal anemia is very common during pregnancy and may develop int severe anemia in about 5–10 percent of pregnant women, increasing materna morbidity and the risk of mortality (Brabin and others 2004). Placental infec tion has been positively associated with low birthweight in newborns, th single greatest risk factor for infant morbidity and mortality, due to intra uterine growth retardation and premature delivery (Brabin and others 2004) In high-transmission areas, primigravidae women and their offspring ar most vulnerable to malaria infection and its adverse health consequence (Menendez 1995). Moreover, the epidemiological evidence accumulate in the past 15 years indicates that HIV-positive pregnant women living in malaria-endemic areas experience higher frequency and higher density o parasitemia, and co-infected women have more febrile illnesses, more anemia and more adverse birth outcomes than women infected with only malaria o HIV (Steketee and others 2001; Ter Kuile and others 2004). Moreover, th efficacy of antimalarials was reported to be compromised in areas with high HIV seroprevalence, requiring higher doses of SP to sufficiently clear infec tions (Parise and others 1998).

The administration of intermittent preventive treatment with SP has prove to be an effective and safe intervention and is highly recommended in high transmission areas as part of routine antenatal care, particularly during firs and second pregnancies (WHO 2004c). However, few pregnant women cu rently benefit from this preventive intervention. Attendance rates in antenata clinics, especially in Sub-Saharan Africa, are low mainly due to househol poverty, poor access to healthcare services, and low quality of care (Molyneu and Nantulya 2004; Nosten and others 2004). Since the 1990s, maternal mo tality rates have increased in Africa because of the HIV/AIDS pandemic an

National malaria control strategies rely primarily on effective case management

the parasite resistance to antimalarials (Nosten and others 2004). The challenge, therefore, is to strengthen antenatal care services to ensure integrated service delivery for appropriate management of both infections. An effective alternative to SP is also required. The efficacy of this antimalarial medicine has reduced significantly because of resistance throughout much of Africa. Free provision of intermittent preventive treatment and insecticide-treated bednets through antenatal care services or other avenues is expected to reduce the burden of malaria in this vulnerable group.

In areas of unstable transmission, adults have relatively little acquired immunity and become symptomatic when infected with *P. falciparum*. Untreated, the infection in pregnant women may cause severe clinical illness. Severe and cerebral malaria during pregnancy is frequent in low-transmission areas (Menendez 1995). Poor pregnancy outcomes such as miscarriage, premature delivery, and stillbirth have been reported frequently as a consequence of acute malaria illness during epidemics and in nonimmune pregnant women (Menendez 1995). In such settings, case management of malaria illness and anemia is a priority, along with the use of insecticide-treated bednets for malaria prevention. The administration of intermittent preventive treatment with antimalarials in areas with seasonal and unstable transmission is not recommended.

Disease management strategies

National malaria control strategies rely primarily on effective case management within the primary healthcare system, especially in Africa, while attempting the large-scale deployment of other interventions such as insecticide-treated bednets and indoor residual spraying. The greatest weakness of this approach is that many malaria-affected populations have low access to diagnostic and treatment services at the onset of their illness; this is especially the case in rural parts of tropical Africa. Furthermore, the quality of curative services (such as shortage of antimalarial medicines and long waiting times) provided by public and private providers often fails to meet the population's health needs. As a result, malaria-affected communities generally resort to self-treatment with inappropriate and poor-quality medicines. In many cases, medicines used for self-treatment are obtained through the unregulated private and informal sectors and are often fake preparations that lack any antimalarial ingredients (Amin and others 2003; Deming and others 1989; Deressam, Ali, and Enqusellassie 2003; Mwenesi, Harpham, and Snow 1995; Ruebush and others 1995; Williams and Jones 2004). Therefore, particular attention must be directed toward increasing access to diagnostic and treatment services, ensuring the supply of antimalarial medicines, and improving the quality of treatment practices at all levels of the healthcare system. A sustained commitment to health systems development is critical for improving case management in malaria-endemic countries.

Community-based interventions improve knowledge, health-seeking behavior, and compliance

The results of a number of surveys indicate that childhood malaria is confronted first at home (Comoro and others 2003; Diallo, De Serres, and Beavogu 2001; Kofoed and others 2004; McCombie 1996). There is a pressing need to promote community-based interventions that will improve local knowledge, health-seeking behavior, and malaria treatment and compliance practices outside the formal healthcare system. Increased emphasis must also be placed on strengthening the healthcare system by expanding service delivery through supporting health extension services. This support should include staff supervision, technical assistance, management, monitoring, and evaluation.

Malaria diagnosis

Effective treatment of malaria cases relies on prompt and accurate diagnosis. The microscopic examination of stained thick and thin blood smears has been the gold standard for diagnosing malaria (Makler, Palmer, and Ager 1998). The cost of material is modest ($0.12–$0.40 per slide), and this method has a high specificity and sensitivity in detecting and identifying malaria parasites. Microscopic examination, however, requires a laboratory setting with electricity, microscopes, and well trained health personnel and about an hour of processing time from blood collection to reporting of results. Most health facilities, especially at the peripheral levels of the health system, cannot meet these requirements. As a result, in resource-poor settings, malaria diagnosis is often based on clinical signs and symptoms.

In the absence of microscopic facilities, particularly in high-transmission areas, all fever episodes are diagnosed as clinical malaria and treated presumptively, especially to reduce mortality in children. The clinical features of malaria, however, are notoriously nonspecific and overlap with those of other common childhood diseases. Therefore, such practice often results in over-treatment with antimalarials and increases operational costs. For instance, a recent study indicated that treatment based on clinical diagnosis would have resulted in unnecessary use of antimalarials in approximately 30 percent of children in a holo-endemic area in Tanzania (Tarimo, Minjas, and Bygbjer 2001). Analysis of data obtained from demographic and health surveys (DHS) and multiple indicator cluster surveys (MICS) from several countries in Africa present similar evidence of a large overuse of antimalarials by children under five years of age based on the presumptive treatment of all fevers (Snow, Ecker, and Teklehaimanot 2003).

Due to increasing parasite resistance, WHO currently recommends a number of combination therapies (see the section on effective and available antimalarials) that are less affordable than commonly used monotherapies and encourages a rapid change in malaria treatment policies in countries where chloroquine and SP are failing. Confirmed diagnosis has therefore become more important today than ever before; routine use of diagnostic tools may reduce the cost of case management to governments and self-medicating

**Rapid
diagnostic
tests should
be used as a
complement
o microscopy**

patient populations, especially in Africa. Nonetheless, the risks associated with making a parasitological diagnosis mandatory in highly endemic areas (such as delays in treatment and a higher child morbidity and mortality) must be carefully weighed against the possible benefits (such as cost savings on combination therapies and work-hours). On the other hand, when malaria transmission is less intense (such as in the highlands and semiarid fringes of Africa and in much of Asia and the Americas), people have little functional immunity to malaria and the presence of malaria parasites is almost always associated with the disease. In such situations, a confirmatory diagnosis of malaria is important prior to antimalarial treatment.

During the past decade, a variety of simple and rapid diagnostic tests have been developed for accurate and reliable malaria diagnosis in settings that lack laboratory facilities, particularly in rural communities. These diagnostic tests—the most user-friendly format is known as a dipstick—detect major antigens derived from malaria parasites using immunochromatographic assays and yield results in 5 to 15 minutes (Wongsrichanalai 2001). The most commonly targeted antigens are the histidine-rich protein 2[1] (HRP2) and the parasite lactate-dehydrogenase[2] (pLDH) (Moody 2002). Several commercial test kits are available today.

Although rapid diagnostic tests are reported to be practical for field use, recently published reviews highlighted the need for improving test sensitivity and specificity, as considerable variations were reported within and across commercial test kits (Makler, Palmer, and Ager 1998; Murray and others 2003; Wongsrichanalai 2001). The sensitivity of recently reviewed rapid diagnostic tests for the detection of *P. falciparum* compared with conventional microscopy range from 35 percent to 97 percent with specificities of 77 percent to 100 percent, whereas for the detection of *P. vivax* the range is from 2 percent to 97 percent with specificities of 97 percent to 100 percent. More specifically, the sensitivity of rapid diagnostic tests at low levels of parasitemia and for nonimmune populations remains a problem. Additional concerns in the development of rapid diagnostic tests include false positivity due to persistent HRP2 antigenemia after parasite clearance and false negativity due to antigen excess at high parasite densities and deletion of HRP2 gene (Moody 2002).

In addition to these technical limitations, a number of feasibility-related issues limit the use of rapid diagnostic tests in malaria endemic areas. The current cost of rapid diagnostic tests ($2–$4 per test) is relatively high compared with the cost of treatment with ACTs (Wongsrichanalai 2001). Commercial test kits currently on the market are not sufficiently robust under routine field conditions (Makler, Palmer, and Ager 1998). Relative sensitivities of rapid diagnostic tests are likely to be influenced by conditions of storage and use.

In high-transmission settings, virtually all residents are parasitemic whether or not they are symptomatic. As a result, parasitemic patients may frequently be "sick with malaria" rather than "sick due to malaria." Detection of parasites

Combination therapy is the way forward for the treatment of malaria

in the blood without concomitant presence of signs and symptoms of malaria illness may therefore be of limited value in the rational use of antimalarial medicines. Under such circumstances, the use of rapid diagnostic tests is not justified, especially in younger groups in whom malaria accounts for a high proportion of fever episodes. Decision to treat should be best left to clinical judgment, given the risk to life of a false negative result by microscopy or rapid diagnostic tests.

At present, the role of rapid diagnostic tests as a diagnostic tool in the management of malaria is limited. These tests should be used as a complement to microscopy. However, rapid diagnostic tests have a recognized, cost-effective role in patient management in areas with unstable malaria transmission where malaria accounts for only a proportion of fevers, and also during malaria epidemics, complex emergencies, and epidemiological surveys. Further research and development is necessary to overcome aforementioned technical and feasibility limitations and enhance the performance of rapid diagnostic tests for reliable diagnosis in different transmission settings.

Effective and available antimalarials

Chloroquine has generally lost its effectiveness in most regions of the world where *P. falciparum* malaria is prevalent (Wongsrichanalai and others 2002). It is important to note that chloroquine-resistant *P. vivax* is now emerging in Myanmar, Guyana, India, Indonesia, and Papua New Guinea (Garg and others 1995; Kyaw and others 1993; Murphy and others 1993; Phillips, Keystone, and Kain 1996; Pukrittayakamee and others 2004; Rieckmann, Davis, and Hutton 1989). Following its widespread introduction as an alternative to chloroquine, SP lost its clinical efficacy in many parts of the world within about five years of its introduction. The loss of clinical efficacy of SP was particularly rapid in East Africa, South America, and Southeast Asia (Sibley and others 2001). In the late 1980s and 1990s, high-level mefloquine resistance rendered most of Southeast Asia and some focal points in the Amazon Basin multimedicine-resistant (Guerin and others 2002).

Failure of our most useful medicines presents a major challenge in malaria control efforts today. Combination therapy, a standard therapeutic practice in other diseases such as tuberculosis, HIV/AIDS, and cancer, is considered the way forward in malaria therapy in spite of its increased costs. Field trials recently showed that ACTs provided effective treatment and markedly reduced resistance development in administered antimalarial medicines (Nosten and Brasseur 2002; Wilairatana and others 2002).

At present, WHO recommends five combination therapies for deployment depending on their efficacy in different geographical areas (box 4.1) (WHO 2001a). Artemether and lumefantrine have been co-formulated into a fixed dose tablet named Coartem®. To date, no resistance has been reported against either component. The rest of the combination therapies are composed

Box 4.1

WHO-recommended combination therapies

- Artemether/lumefantrine
- Artesunate + amodiaquine
- Artesunate + SP
- Artesunate + mefloquine
- Amodiaquine + SP

Source: WHO 2001a.

independently acting antimalarial components that should be co-administered to malaria patients. These combination therapies are suggested for the treatment of malaria in areas where all components remain effective. Artesunate (another artisiminin derivative) combined with mefloquine is currently recommended for treatment only in low- to moderate-transmission areas. The fifth and last option, amodiaquine plus SP, is a nonartemisinin therapy that may be deployed in West Africa where efficacy of both antimalarials remains high.

During the past three years, 39 endemic countries have updated their treatment policies and have adopted one of these five combination therapies (RBM 2004). In Africa, Benin, Burundi, Cameroon, Comores, Ethiopia, Equatorial Guinea, Gabon, Ghana Kenya, São Tomé and Principé, South Africa, Tanzania, Uganda, and Zambia have adopted ACTs. Mozambique, Rwanda, and Senegal have switched to amodiaquine plus SP. Implementation within the public health sector, however, remains weak. In Africa only 5 countries, and outside Africa only 10, are deploying these antimalarial medicines (as of mid-2004). In the interim, a number of countries are attempting to buy time by using a nonfixed combination of existing medicines such as chloroquine plus SP or amodiaquine plus SP. The decision to continue with these medicines in the face of reduced treatment efficacy is largely because of financial constraints.

With the introduction of combination therapies, a two-pronged case management strategy has been proposed based on microscopic diagnosis at the more central levels of the healthcare system (such as district hospitals) and rapid diagnostic tests in remote communities or highly mobile populations at peripheral health posts. Rapid diagnostic tests are expected to increase the performance and work quality of community health workers, particularly in areas of unstable transmission. In high-transmission areas, the use of rapid diagnostic tests can be effective, provided they complement clinical diagnosis to target treatment to those who are clinically ill.

Malaria management at home

Health service coverage in many African countries is inadequate, and rural populations generally lack access to basic healthcare services. In addition, the delivery of medicine and other essential commodities, particularly to rural communities, is not always reliable. Service agencies often run out of

Community-based strategies must be promoted to improve malaria diagnosis and treatment

essential medicines such as antimalarials. These factors, coupled with prob lems of accessibility and affordability, pose major obstacles and disincentive to use healthcare services in rural populations. Rural populations often reso to self-medication with antimalarial medicines obtained from the unregulate informal sector or traditional healers. The delivery of prepackaged antimalaria medicines would facilitate their use at the household and community level an may improve compliance.

An RBM survey, undertaken as part of a situation analysis in several Africa countries, indicated that between 70 percent and 90 percent of febrile childre are treated at home. Therefore, there is an urgent need to address the issu of treatment for uncomplicated malaria at the community level. A number endemic countries are seeking to improve their healthcare coverage by extendin health services beyond the formal health service infrastructure through the us of networks of village health workers. Communities often readily accept th approach because mothers and caregivers can obtain prompt access to effectiv medicines and counseling within the local community. These community-base strategies have been shown to reduce severe morbidity and under-five mortali in malaria endemic areas (Chahnazarian and others 1993; Ghebreyesus ar others 1996; Kidane and Morrow 2000; Pagnoni and others 1997).

If the targets set at the Abuja summit are to be realized, particular atten tion must be paid to the large-scale introduction of innovative strategies, suc as the deployment of community health workers for malaria diagnosis an treatment services. Effective case management through community-based in tiatives must be supported by a well functioning healthcare system that pr vides technical support and guidance in handling referred cases.

Epidemic prevention and control strategies

Malaria epidemics are characterized by a sudden and large increase in malar infections and are often associated with high case fatality rates in the com munity. There are several factors that support the development of epidemic The introduction of the disease into previously malaria-free areas, migratio and displacement of nonimmune people into malaria endemic regions, or a unusual increase in vector abundance caused by climate anomalies may trigg explosive epidemics (Worrall, Rietveld, and Delacollette 2004). In Afric most malaria epidemics are climate driven and frequently occur in semiar and highland areas of the eastern and southern parts of the continent, whe malaria transmission is unstable (that is, seasonal), and people have little no immunity against the disease (Kiszewski and Teklehaimanot 2004). Su climate-driven epidemics generally occur in two- to seven-year cycles, followin the periodicity of abnormal meteorological conditions (Worrall, Rietveld, a Delacollette 2004).

Although the health burden of epidemic malaria has not been adequate documented, it is known to be very large, particularly in Africa (map 4.1).

Map 4.1

Malaria epidemics between 1997 and 2002 added to a heavy health burden in Africa

Source: World Health Organization.

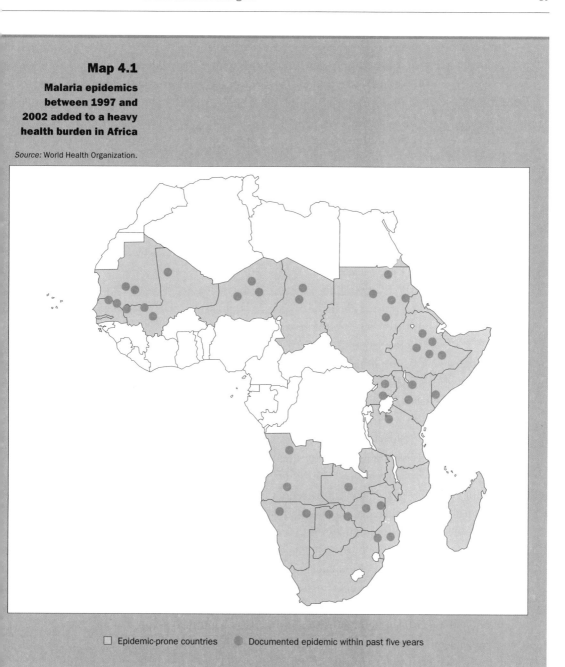

☐ Epidemic-prone countries ⬤ Documented epidemic within past five years

unstable transmission areas, case fatality rates can be up to 10 times higher during outbreaks than in nonepidemic conditions (Kiszewski and Tekle-haimanot 2004). Some 110 million people in Africa coexist with epidemic malaria (WHO and UNICEF 2003). Although epidemics may occur in iso-lated pockets, they may at times be widespread and catastrophic. For example, the malaria epidemic that occurred in Ethiopia in 1958 caused an estimated 3 million clinical cases, resulting in some 150,000 deaths (Fontaine, Najjar, and Prince 1961). A number of factors may exacerbate the deleterious effects of

Malaria epidemics are associated with high case fatality rates and heavy economic losses

malaria epidemics. Specifically, fragile health systems in many African coun-tries become overwhelmed during malaria epidemics, when both inpatient and outpatient capacities are surpassed. Under such conditions, the provision of routine health services and record keeping diminishes, creating ripple effects in the health systems that extend beyond the epidemic period (Kiszewski and Teklehaimanot 2004).

In addition to the direct health burden, epidemic malaria results in heavy economic losses, at both household and community levels, due to lost produc-tivity. In many rural communities of Africa, epidemics strike during planting and harvesting seasons when the demand for labor is greatest (Kiszewski and Teklehaimanot 2004). Economic activities are also likely to be adversely affected by epidemics or the threat of epidemics (Worrall, Rietveld, and Dela-collette 2004).

Intervention strategies directed against epidemics should include a detailed study of potential triggering mechanisms at the local level for forecasting and early detection of malaria outbreaks (WHO 2004a). It is essential that capacity for data collection, analysis, and utilization be developed within the minis-tries of health in malaria-affected countries. Such data will be used to inform intersectoral collaborative efforts for rapid assessment and early containment of epidemics. Early warning and forecasting with effective surveillance systems can reduce the adverse effects of malaria epidemics significantly through pre-paredness and prevention (Thomson and Connor 2001).

It is important to be cognizant of the role that nonclimatic factors (such as war, migration, and changes in local vector ecology due to human activity) play in the development of malaria epidemics. These and other social and envi-ronmental factors should be taken into account to accurately predict and deter malaria outbreaks (Connor, Thomson, and Molyneux 1999; Teklehaimanot and others 2004; Thomson and Connor 2001). In the event that a malaria epi-demic is detected and confirmed, indoor residual spraying should be deployed to effectively curtail transmission, and insecticide-treated bednets should be distributed. Along with vector control measures, febrile cases should be rapidly screened and treated with effective antimalarial medicines.

Information, education, and communication strategies

Community participation is the process by which local residents influence the decisions and allocation of resources that directly affect them. In this context, information, education, and communication and social mobilization consti-tute crucial components of successful malaria control programs. There are many examples of how strong community-based action has functioned as a first-line defense against malaria (WHO 2002).

Information, education, and communication components should be sensi-tive to local sociocultural and environmental variables and should foster a sense of ownership by all involved. Such an approach requires that the responsibili-

Malaria control efforts should be integrated with other health programs

for the program be distributed broadly across all participatory levels. All concerned parties must understand the goals of the program and be sensitive to potential points of friction that may prevent successful implementation. Collaboration should be sought and established among personnel and institutions already operating in the community in order to integrate local actors into new malaria control efforts.

Furthermore, malaria control efforts should be integrated with other health programs—such as those concerned with tuberculosis, HIV/AIDS, and safe motherhood—to foster effective and efficient horizontal communication (Moerman and others 2003). Adapting malaria control programs to the local context is crucial, and intervention strategies should be worked out and agreed upon in concert with the affected communities. Personnel with experience in information, education, and communication activities, and those with appropriate language and communication skills and a solid knowledge of the sociocultural, political, and economic characteristics of the community should be engaged in guiding such efforts (Njama and others 2003). Such an approach requires more than simply imparting knowledge from healthcare officials to community members; rather it encompasses a broad exchange and adapting of implementation measures to the needs of each individual community.

Monitoring and evaluation

The success of malaria control strategies depends in large part on how these strategies are implemented in the local context. Monitoring and evaluation are essential activities in program implementation, both to identify the appropriate mix of malaria control interventions and to assess the effectiveness of program activities over time. At all levels of malaria endemicity, malaria control programs should monitor trends in malaria morbidity and mortality, resistance to antimalarial medicines, and coverage rates of key interventions for malaria prevention and management. The specific indicators to be used in monitoring should be chosen according to local transmission conditions. For example, in high-transmission settings, insecticide-treated bednet coverage for children under five years of age, intermittent preventive treatment use in pregnant women, and prompt treatment of child fevers with effective antimalarials would be appropriate outcome indicators. In epidemic-prone areas, insecticide-treated bednet use across all age groups and prompt deployment of indoor residual spraying during epidemics may be among the outcome indicators chosen for monitoring. Other essential outcomes for monitoring include the availability and distribution of important malaria commodities such as antimalarial medicines.

The central challenge to monitoring and evaluation activities is their dependence on the consistent availability of high-quality data for chosen indicators. At present, most national malaria control programs in Africa conduct program monitoring and evaluation based on data from national health information

Information systems for health should integrate facility-level and community-level data

systems. These data have important limitations, however. National health information systems do not capture detailed data on important malaria outcome indicators because they collect data only from patients seen in government health service facilities, thereby excluding large segments of the rural population who do not have access to health facilities.

A number of surveys have been developed and widely implemented to obtain health information on populations that reside outside health service coverage areas, and on outcome indicators that may not be routinely collected in national health information systems. These surveys will be described in detail in chapter 8; among them are those developed specifically for malaria monitoring. These surveys provide population-based health data. Information systems for health should be modernized and strengthened and, as resources for health increase, should integrate facility-level and community-level data in a cohesive manner.

Chapter 5

Examples of successful scale-up of malaria control programs

Malaria-related success in Africa has been limited by an acute shortage of trained health personnel, underdeveloped health systems, and lack of adequate funding and effective organization. The difficulties in implementing malaria control programs in this continent are compounded by climatic and biological factors. African mosquitoes have greater capacity as malaria vectors than other *Anopheles* mosquitoes. Endemicity in Africa, therefore, is particularly intense.

Examples of the successful scale-up of malaria control activities can be found in Ethiopia, Madagascar, Viet Nam, South Africa, and Tanzania. The experiences of these successful programs, reviewed in this chapter, reveal that sustained reductions in the malaria burden can be achieved when malaria control programs are implemented through well coordinated efforts that span the national and regional levels. Successful implementation was achieved through the availability of appropriate funding from development partners.

The main feature of these successful programs is the deployment of an integrated package of effective malaria control interventions, tailored to the local context, along with effective program monitoring and evaluation. Two districts in Tanzania have also demonstrated that optimum utilization of funds can achieve the desired results in terms of morbidity and mortality reduction. Thus, the following case studies demonstrate the feasibility of effective control with scaled-up malaria control programs and describe the common factors for their success. The Eritrean Malaria Control Program policy of free distribution of insecticide-treated nets combined with community-based case management has resulted in a significant increase in insecticide-treated net coverage and marked reduction in malaria cases (Graves 2004).

The main feature of successful programs is an integrated package of effective malaria control interventions

Tigray region of Ethiopia

Due to its varied ecological and epidemiological features, Ethiopia is intensely affected by destructive malaria epidemics that occur at regular intervals. The epidemic that struck northern Ethiopia in 1958 devastated the region, resulting in 150,000 deaths and some 3 million clinical cases (Fontaine, Najjar, and Prince 1961). Alarmed by the magnitude of the disaster, the national government launched a malaria control program in 1961. This program included case management, the use of indoor residual spraying, limited use of environmental management, and establishment of an extensive surveillance network. Indoor residual spraying with DDT, with an annual coverage of some eight million people, remains one of the main modes of intervention in the country. Over the past decades, malaria epidemics have continued to occur, but at reduced levels of severity.

The Tigray region of northern Ethiopia is populated by about four million people, 75 percent of whom reside in areas vulnerable to malaria outbreaks. Less than half of the population lives within 10 kilometers of a health center. The rest of the population does not have access to healthcare services. In addition to regular indoor residual spraying campaigns and case management services at health centers, the regional government of Tigray introduced a community-based malaria intervention strategy in 1992 to provide regionwide and sustained access to early diagnosis and treatment and to promptly identify and confine malaria outbreaks (WHO 1999).

As part of this community-based approach, a package of interventions was adopted that included home management of cases by training mothers and local village volunteers. The success of the program was made possible largely because of the region's well established social system and strong commitment to community involvement, which served as a backdrop to establishing a network of 700 volunteer health workers. These volunteer health workers were assigned the tasks of social mobilization, implementation of source reduction measures, clinical diagnosis, and treatment at the village level (Alemayehu, Ghebreyesus, and others 1998; Alemayehu, Ye-ebiyo, and others 1998).

More than a half million people received free treatment for malaria each year through this network of volunteer health workers (WHO 1999). District health management teams and malaria control program personnel provided technical support, supervision, and free distribution of antimalarial medicines. Insecticide-treated net use was also promoted. All of the villages in the region were mapped using global positioning systems (GPS). Geographic information systems (GIS), including HealthMapper software, was used in the analysis of surveillance data and malaria trends.

The community-based approach, which has been expanded over the years, has shifted the bulk of diagnosis and treatment to the community health workers (figure 5.1). Extension of coverage of early diagnosis and treatment to the periphery has been a major success and is partly responsible for the increase

Figure 5.1

The number of treated malaria patients at different healthcare levels has risen from 1992 to 1998 in the Tigray region of Ethiopia

Treated patients (thousands)

Source: WHO 1999.

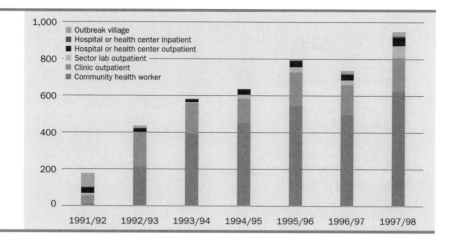

in the number of malaria patients treated since the start of the program. Community-based malaria program activities are likely to have contributed to the observed 40 percent reduction in the overall under-five child mortality rate from 1994 to 1996 (WHO 1999).

Highlands of Madagascar

DDT spraying of houses and mass chemoprophylaxis of schoolchildren with chloroquine led to the disappearance of the malaria vector *A. funestus* and malaria in the highlands of Madagascar in the 1950s and 1960s (Joncour 1956). In the mid-1970s, *A. funestus* returned slowly to the highlands due to reduced vector control programs, which resulted in a series of malaria epidemics that broke out between 1985 and 1990, killing tens of thousands of people (Lepers and others 1990).

Malaria rates reaching pre-eradication levels incited the government to mobilize a campaign against malaria in 1989 (Pietra and others 2002). The program, known as the Opération de Pulvérisation Intra-Domiciliaire (OPID), was funded in large part through the World Bank and consisted of five vector control campaigns that focused on areas located in epidemic zones. The program included community-level distribution of chloroquine. From 1994 to 1998 the program was extended to cover nearly all of the epidemic-prone highland areas of the island. The combined use of chloroquine and DDT protected 2.3 million inhabitants per year and resulted in the satisfactory containment of malaria between 1993 and 2000 (map 5.1).

The pre-OPID parasite prevalence in a sample of villages in the highlands (1,000–1,500 meters) was 23.8 percent; post-OPID (1998–2000) this rate had been reduced to 0.4 percent (Romi and others 2002). In 1997, an epidemiologic surveillance and warning system was put in place that supports the application of indoor residual spraying for epidemic control (Curtis 2002a; Romi and others 2002). Currently, the national malaria control program is promoting the use of insecticide-treated nets and is planning to improve malaria diagnosis

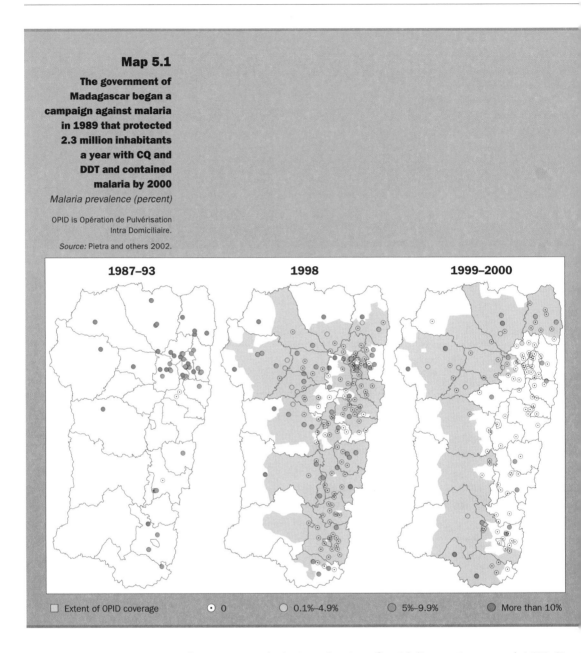

Map 5.1

The government of Madagascar began a campaign against malaria in 1989 that protected 2.3 million inhabitants a year with CQ and DDT and contained malaria by 2000

Malaria prevalence (percent)

OPID is Opération de Pulvérisation Intra Domiciliaire.

Source: Pietra and others 2002.

1987–93   1998   1999–2000

☐ Extent of OPID coverage   ⊙ 0   ○ 0.1%–4.9%   ○ 5%–9.9%   ● More than 10%

and treatment with the introduction of rapid diagnostic tests and ACTs (Ran drianarivelojosia 2004).

Viet Nam

In Viet Nam, a Southeast Asian country of 81 million people, as much as third of the population resides in malaria-affected areas. Although the countr has historically been affected by malaria, the disease was successfully cor tained from 1978 to 1985. In the late 1980s, the situation began to deteriorat because of a number of factors. Vector control operations came to a stand still because donations of DDT from the Soviet Union ceased. Furthermore the commonly used antimalarial medicines proved to be virtually ineffective because of high levels of medicine resistance. Finally, large-scale population movements enhanced conditions for the development of malaria epidemics.

In 1991, 144 outbreaks were recorded, affecting more than one million people. Alarmed by the worsening situation, the Vietnamese government increased its investment in malaria control and adopted a package of interventions that included free distribution and treatment of bednets in annual or biannual campaigns, application of indoor residual spraying in areas where people did not have a habit of using bednets, and deployment of new antimalarial medicines, including artemisinin derivatives. There was a major investment in training and supervision, and 400 mobile teams were set up by the Ministry of Health to supervise voluntary health workers on measures to improve health-seeking behavior at the community level. The number of people protected by vector control methods (that is, the use of insecticide-treated nets and the application of indoor residual spraying) increased from 4 million in 1991 to 12 million by 1998. Specifically, the number of people using insecticide-treated nets rose from 300,000 to more than 10 million.

This integrated package of interventions was evaluated over a five-year period (1992 until 1997). Mortality and morbidity rates were reduced by 97 percent and 60 percent respectively (figure 5.2). Local malaria outbreaks were virtually eliminated (WHO 2000b).

South Africa

In South Africa malaria is confined primarily to the northeast regions of the country, in the Limpopo, Mpumalanga, and KwaZulu-Natal provinces. The success of the country's malaria control program is the direct result of an approach based on an integrated package of interventions, which consist mainly of vector control measures and antimalarial treatments. In general, these provinces have enjoyed strong political support from the government and the Southern Africa Development Community in combating malaria (Balfour 2002).

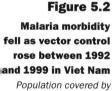

Figure 5.2

Malaria morbidity fell as vector control rose between 1992 and 1999 in Viet Nam

Population covered by spraying, insecticide-treated bednets (millions)

Source: WHO 2000b.

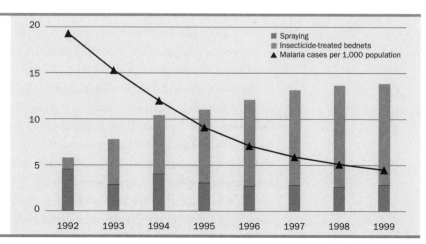

The history of malaria control in South Africa can briefly be summarize
as follows (Musawenkosi, Sharp, and Lengeler 2004):

- 1930s: First application of indoor residual spraying using pyrethrun
  against lethal epidemics occuring as far south as Durban.
- Early 1940s: Beginning of the manufacture of DDT in South Afric.
  South African DDT was used in the antityphus measures in Naples i
  1943.
- Late 1940s: Beginning of the application of indoor residual sprayin
  with DDT in 1946, followed by significant reduction in malaria-relate
  morbidity and mortality.
- 1950s: *A. funestus,* one of the target malaria vectors, disappeared und
  DDT pressure.
- 1995: Decision in South Africa (but not Swaziland) to discontinu
  DDT (despite continued susceptibility of the vector *A. arabiensis* to i
  and switch to indoor residual spraying with pyrethroid deltamethrin.
- 1990s: Detection of 80 percent resistance of *P. falciparum* to SP an
  decision to switch to ACTs in South Africa (Bredenkamp and othe
  2001).
- 2000: Quadrupling of the malaria incidence since 1995, associated wit
  re-emergence of *A. funestus* (presumably from Mozambique). Loc.
  A. funestus populations were shown by bioassays to be resistant to pyr
  throids but not to DDT (Hargreaves and others 2000).
- 2000: Decision to switch back to DDT spraying in daub houses bu
  not in plastered houses, where visible DDT deposits are considere
  unacceptable. At the final round of negotiations on the Convention c
  Persistent Organic Pollutants the South African delegation proposed
  carefully worded amendment to allow continued use of DDT for vect
  control. The amendment was unanimously adopted by a plenary neg
  tiating session representing 150 nations.
- 2002: In KwaZulu-Natal Province malaria incidence declined by 9
  percent from the incidence observed in 2000. Although low levels c
  DDT resistance were detected for the first time in *A. arabiensis,* th
  vector was successfully eliminated by intensive pyrethroid spraying.

The establishment of the Lubombo Spatial Development Initiative (LSD
by the governments of Mozambique, South Africa, and Swaziland has accele
ated the campaign against malaria on a regional basis. The LSDI is a uniqu
collaboration between the three countries that aims to transform the L+momb
region into an economically competitive zone. To this end, the malaria burde
was identified as a major barrier and a Regional Malaria Control Commissio
was created to oversee malaria control efforts.

Malaria incidence has been steadily decreasing in the Lubombo regic
since 2000, and the contiguous area under malaria control now covers approx
mately 100,000 square kilometers in the three countries (LSDI 2004). The u

of indoor residual spraying has been extended to the whole region, and ACT implementation is well under way. While 41,786 cases of malaria were reported in KwaZulu-Natal province in 2000, there were only 9,443 cases in 2001, corresponding to a 78 percent reduction during the first year of implementation (MSF 2003). In particular, the provinces of Kwa-Zulu Natal and Mpumalanga recorded 96 percent and 75 percent reductions in the number of malaria cases during the period between 2000 and 2003, respectively, whereas the incidence of malaria decreased by 91 percent in Swaziland (LSDI 2004). As of June 2004, malaria prevalence in children decreased by 89 percent and 76 percent in zones 1 and 1A, respectively, in Mozambique (map 5.2).

The integrated approach to malaria control has been the key to the reduction of malaria incidence in the Lubombo region (LSDI 2004). Continued success has been achieved by maintaining an appropriate skills base among malaria control personnel in the region and by ensuring the program's financial sustainability. Initial financing came from the South African Business Trust and MOZAL (Mozambique Aluminum); private sector funding constituted 100 percent of funding in the first two years. However, by the fourth year of the project, the public-to-private ratio of funding was 50:50, with the Mozambique and South African governments increasing their contributions. This regional malaria control initiative was awarded a GFATM allocation in 2003 (LSDI 2004).

Tanzania

Starting out as an integrated research and development project in Rufiji and Morogoro Districts of Tanzania in 1997, the Tanzanian Essential Health Interventions Project (TEHIP) has observed significant reductions in the mortality of children under the age of five when districts used an evidence-based approach to health planning (figure 5.3). These districts are actually well on track to meet the Millennium Development Goal target for under-five mortality rate reductions 10 years ahead of schedule. This success has shown that "a major constraint of the District Health System was not just the money available, but the capacity to spend it" (IDRC/TEHIP 2004). The inner workings of the TEHIP project are described in box 5.1 (De Savigny and others 2004).

In the districts of Rufiji and Morogoro in Tanzania, Demographic Surveillance Systems (DSS) provide the sentinel information base for monitoring the full scope of health problems at the household level and feeding this into district-level health planning. Analogous DSS information systems also operate at the district level in 19 countries, mostly in Sub-Saharan Africa and Asia, including parts of Bangladesh, Burkina Faso, Ghana, Indonesia, Mozambique, South Africa, Senegal, and Viet Nam. With monitoring and surveillance systems in place, and using simple tools for interpreting the evidence for district planners, existing district-level health budgets can be better allocated according to local

Map 5.2

Malaria incidence and prevalence in the Lubombo region is reduced by indoor residual spraying with effective insecticides and the use of effective treatment (ACT)

Source: LSDI 2004.

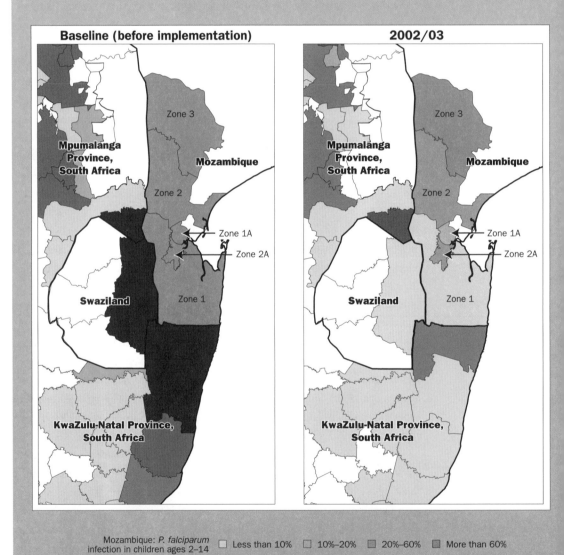

Mozambique: *P. falciparum* infection in children ages 2–14   ☐ Less than 10%   ☐ 10%–20%   ▨ 20%–60%   ▩ More than 60%

South Africa; Lubombo District, Swaziland: Malaria incidence per 1,000 population   ☐ 0.01–1.5   ☐ 1.5–3.0   ▨ 3.0–6.0   ■ 6.0–18.0   ■ More than 18   ☐ No data

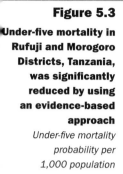

Figure 5.3

Under-five mortality in Rufuji and Morogoro Districts, Tanzania, was significantly reduced by using an evidence-based approach

Under-five mortality probability per 1,000 population

Source: IDRC/TEHIP 2004.

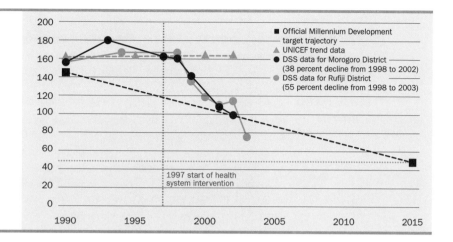

health priorities. This facilitates setting feasible burden reduction targets for the most important and tractable problems appropriate to the local district-level situation.

Experience to date, as in the TEHIP program in Tanzania, indicates that such sentinel community-level information systems can provide the basis for bringing about much more rational allocation of existing and new district-level funds and personnel to better focus resources on the highest disease burden, with dramatic reductions in, for example, the mortality of children under the age of five, in short order (see figure 5.3).

The prioritization of health interventions according to local morbidity and mortality burdens also made transparent what additional funds—beyond government allocations—and capacity building would be necessary in the short run to bring about substantial declines, as illustrated above, in under-five mortality. A recent assessment of the effectiveness of the district health services in malaria control in another part of Tanzania, where such priority setting and resource allocation tools have not been used, has concluded that insufficient capacity to develop local policies that reflect local needs and resources, and the lack of a local malaria control strategy, resulted in limited success in reducing malaria at the district level (Alilio and others 2004). The general principle, of which the TEHIP program is exemplary, is that systemic interventions that strengthen health systems to do a better job of delivering key health interventions can significantly contribute to the Millennium Development Goals progress as long as local ownership, decentralized control of resources, and steadily increasing funding are provided for scaling up (IDRC/TEHIP 2004).

Starting this kind of process on the broadest feasible scale in the short run could initiate a longer term process that would meet certain health-related Millennium Development Goals targets in a timely fashion. A top priority should be to immediately initiate such district-level systemic health system improvements in what may be regarded as the beginning stage of a substantial scaling-up process.

Box 5.1

District-level health intervention systems in Tanzania

Source: IDRC/TEHIP 2004.

Through continuous sentinel population health and mortality surveillance in Tanzania, vital statistics (such as births, deaths, migrations, and causes of deaths) are updated regularly to generate profiles of the annual burden of disease for districts. These profiles of intervention priorities, coupled with an appreciation of district-level capacity and community preferences, inform priority setting and budget allocations that lead to a greater push on cost-effective interventions that address the largest shares of the disease burden actually experienced by local communities. For instance, malaria was shown to be responsible for 30 percent of the years of life lost in the Southern Tanzania DSS sentinel area in 1996. As a result, the Morogoro Council health management teams increased their spending on malaria prevention and treatment from 5 to 25 percent of the health budget the following year (IDRC/TEHIP 2004). Based on surveillance data, health impacts are rigorously monitored at the household level to assess program effectiveness. Tracking the trends in health-seeking behavior, these tools help the health management teams to improve and expand the delivery and use of essential health interventions such as insecticide-treated nets and tuberculosis DOTS treatments in both pilot districts.

A joint venture between the Canadian International Development Research Centre and the Tanzanian Ministry of Health, TEHIP initially increased the per capita health budget from $8 to $10 by offering an unconstrained $2 "basket" of decentralized funds to the districts between 1997 and 2000 to facilitate investment in packages of interventions consistent with the pattern of the local burden of disease (IDRC/TEHIP 2004). However, the incremental per capita spending from these TEHIP funds averaged less than $1 in the pilot districts. Starting in 2001, TEHIP's external financial support was gradually decreased as funding from the new, sectorwide government/donor partnership "basket" grants had started flowing into the district budget. The government of Tanzania supports the scaling up of the TEHIP planning tools and strategies to national level; however, this process is going slowly because of a shortage of financial and human resources for training districts in new approaches.

Lessons learned

The examples cited above illustrate how integrated packages of antimalarial interventions, when implemented on the regional or national level, can bring about significant and sustained reductions in the malaria burden. These examples show the impact of locally relevant, multifaceted malaria programs in diverse situations in malaria-endemic areas, and emphasize that no single intervention strategy can resolve the problem presented by malaria. The salient features common to these programs are:

- The appropriate selection of a locally adapted package of interventions.
- An effective system for monitoring program activities and evaluating impact.

The particular strengths of each program provide guidance in how successful scale-up may be carried out. For example, active participation by the members of affected communities greatly enhanced clinical management of malaria in the Ethiopian program, while a strong emphasis on evidence-based planning led to significant improvements in malaria program management in Tanzania. Successes in malaria control not featured in the examples given here include case management at home and in remote villages in parts of Burkina Faso, the Democratic Republic of Congo, Kenya, and Uganda; and free distribution of prepackaged (chloroquine plus SP) combination medicines in Uganda. The programs featured in this chapter are notable examples of the successful scale-up of malaria control to the regional or national level. Our challenge now is to apply the principles derived from these success stories throughout malaria-endemic countries.

Chapter 6

Priority challenges for scaling up malaria control programs

A range of proven antimalarial tools and interventions exist to prevent, treat, and control malaria. Evidence shows that effective and sustained implementation of existing interventions can significantly reduce malaria-related morbidity and mortality in endemic countries. Successful implementation in the Tigray region of Ethiopia and in Madagascar and Viet Nam was achieved because human and financial resources were made available by development partners. These countries used the funding available to them to launch an integrated package of effective interventions to those at risk of malaria on a large scale. Unfortunately, most malaria control programs are carried out with limited coverage and scope, especially in Africa. To date, these fragmented efforts have not made an impact on the burden that malaria imposes on society.

It is therefore critical to identify key implementation and programmatic challenges to scaling up malaria control programs to national levels. To this end, priority implementation challenges fall broadly into four categories: health systems capacity, human resources capacity, social mobilization of communities, and partnership. The health system constraints are discussed within the context of malaria control programs, along with programmatic challenges at the implementation level.

1. Health systems capacity
   - Inadequate, poor quality, and underused health infrastructure and services, especially in rural areas.
   - Weak health information systems and limited government capacity for surveillance, monitoring, evaluation, and regulation.
   - Inappropriate sectoral policies on expenditure allocations and targeting across levels of care, failing to address social inequalities.

A range of proven antimalarial tools and interventions exist to prevent, treat, and control malaria

- Inappropriate sectoral policies influenced by donor agencies and international organizations that impede free distribution of essential health commodities to endemic populations that are key components of the effective interventions.
- Weak integration, coordination, and collaboration at higher levels of the health system (such as ministries of health), focusing on day-to-day management instead of stewardship in management and strategic planning.
- Insufficient and unsustainable financial investment for strengthening of health systems in developing countries.

2. Human resources capacity
   - Shortage of adequate human resources for planning, implementation, service delivery, monitoring, and evaluation.
   - Inadequate human resource policies on training and compensation, leading to poor performance, absenteeism, emigration, and loss of staff to less poor urban areas or the private sector.

3. Social mobilization of communities
   - Weak community participation in governance and management of local health facilities.
   - Weak community demand for healthcare services due to extreme poverty, low geographical access, and lack of knowledge of prevention and treatment services.

4. Partnerships
   - Low collaboration and weak coordination with the private health sector, NGOs, and civil society organizations to improve coverage and quality of primary healthcare services, especially in rural underserved communities.
   - Little intersectoral activity with other agencies going beyond the ministry of health to increase impact, including other government ministries and the private sector.
   - Unpredictable and low development assistance to the health sector by the donor community, with high transaction costs.

There are some anxieties about the possible undesirable effects of economic globalization on the general health sector, including malaria control. Drugs and other commodities have been available in most developed countries at inexpensive prices because their provision has been subsidized by governments. With the introduction of Trade-Related Aspects of Intellectual Property Rights (TRIPS) and the subsequent requirement for aligning domestic patent laws with the commitments under TRIPS, there will be a change in the scale of the restrictions regulating manufacturing of new drugs and other commodities. The introduction of a TRIPS-consistent patent regime for medicines in a developing country will likely result in an increase in the cost of medicines and services worldwide.

The effective implementation of malaria control interventions rests on the health personnel who manage programs

Strengthening health systems

To ensure the greatest effectiveness and sustainability of malaria control efforts, interventions should be integrated into a strong and functional health system. The UN Millennium Project considers strong health systems to be a *sine qua non* for meeting the health and other Millennium Development Goals. The UN Millennium Project (2005) report *Investing in Development: A Practical Plan to Achieve the Millennium Development Goals* details some of the emerging recommendations for strengthening health systems to accelerate progress toward the Goals. In the following sections, we summarize the aspects of health systems that are essential to malaria control.

Rigorous assessments of existing policies on malaria control and program organization in relation to the general health system should be carried out as part of designing appropriate malaria control programs. The health systems of each country, including health-related institutions, must be up to date on the availability and efficacy of malaria control interventions and the best modes of their deployment. A comprehensive malaria control effort should include a thorough assessment of the existing infrastructure and the capacity and performance of the following program components within the health system:

- Functioning laboratory facilities for diagnosis at different healthcare levels.
- Efficiency of medicine procurement, supply, and distribution systems.
- Adequate number of health staff trained in disease management.
- Operational quality of health information and management systems.
- Facilities for quality assurance and monitoring of substandard or fake medicines, diagnostics, insecticides, and other reagents.
- Systems to monitor medicine and insecticide efficacy to inform policy decisions for appropriate action.
- Supervision and monitoring systems to improve the health workforce performance.
- Availability of quality regulatory and enforcement agencies.
- Policy on free distribution of antimalarial medicines and insecticide treated nets.
- Availability of services offered through antenatal care services and outreach facilities.
- Availability of functioning referral systems for severe malaria cases.

Human resources capacity

The effective implementation of malaria control interventions rests on the availability, the skills, the attitudes, and the motivation of health personnel who manage programs, deliver interventions, and assess their impact. Evidence suggests that countries with the highest disease burden have the lowest health staff per population ratios. Most of them are low-income countries in Africa. Success requires developing human resources through training and certification

Community-level workers are vital for promoting social mobilization and health-seeking behavior

in various disciplines. Required areas of expertise include managing programs; harnessing evidence for effective policymaking and stewardship; capturing developments in best practices for program formulation and intervention development; integrating such best practices into national strategy and guidelines; implementation and monitoring of programs; assessing the impact of interventions; and data management and analytical skills. Acquiring special skills to undertake studies on antimalarial therapeutic efficacy, insecticide susceptibility of vector mosquitoes, and vector ecology and behavior is also critical to implement successful programs. These highly qualified personnel can contribute strongly to regional malaria control efforts. Local training programs administered by trained personnel will provide the necessary skilled workforce for effective implementation at subnational levels.

Community-level health workers such as health extension workers, community health workers, and traditional birth attendants involved in malaria control efforts are trained by ministries of health, bilateral development partners, NGOs, and civil society organizations in a system designed to stimulate their enthusiasm and prepare them for the challenges presented by their communities. These community-level workers are vital for promoting social mobilization and health-seeking behavior and for mobilizing political and financial support.

Social mobilization of communities

Increased awareness and knowledge about healthy behaviors and practices by communities are fundamental for general health promotion, preventing malaria infection, and effective case management. Strategies for social mobilization should be developed at district and peripheral levels. Key elements in such strategies should include promoting community awareness; demanding services that would lead to the adoption of essential disease-prevention attitudes—such as the correct use of insecticide-treated nets and other preventive measures, and improved treatment-seeking behavior—and compliance with prescribed treatments. Health workers in general, especially those at the periphery, are inadequately prepared for mobilizing local communities and sustaining their interest in antimalarial measures.

Control initiatives should seek to empower communities by increasing their awareness and improving health worker skills and practices concerning malaria prevention and treatment. The needs and requirements of particular countries and districts should be considered when developing strategies, training materials, and mechanisms for creating an adequately skilled workforce to support social mobilization.

Partnerships

Malaria-endemic countries, particularly in Africa, have been struggling to combat the burden of malaria with limited human and financial resources,

Most low-income countries are unlikely to achieve their health targets on their own

poor infrastructure, and underdeveloped health systems. Because of such constraints, most malaria programs operate against daunting implementation challenges, rendering them time-limited projects that are unable to bring about a measurable impact on malaria-related morbidity and mortality. At this rate of investment and coverage and quality of health services, these countries on their own will not be able to achieve the Millennium Development Goals for health, including the malaria target, by 2015.

Support from the international donor community for malaria control efforts in Africa during the past five decades was at a minimum at best. Participation was limited to project level. In recent years, however, international donor agencies have become more willing to partner with malaria-endemic countries. The availability of additional funding from the Global Fund to Fight AIDS, Tuberculosis, and Malaria (GFATM) and the level of political support and commitment for the Millennium Development Goals are encouraging for forging constructive partnerships. Private sources such as foundations and corporations have become important in financing global public goods, usually in partnership with multilateral organizations.

While some countries have set goals and targets in line with the Millennium Development Goals for health, they are unlikely to achieve their target unless there is a massive and sustained increase in development assistance from the developed countries to build national capacity. Particularly, financial investment in malaria control has been insufficient, and even endemic countries that are supported by the GFATM have achieved only limited coverage. Partnerships between endemic countries and the developed world are critical if the Millennium Development Goal target on malaria is to be realized by 2015.

Malaria-endemic countries are expected to develop evidence-based national plans with a policy framework, core indicators, and data collection, analysis, and dissemination strategies and to pursue their implementation on a national scale in a transparent and accountable manner. Likewise, the donor community is expected to mobilize the necessary resources to fund nationwide control programs. The partnership should not be seen as benefiting only one side, but as a collaborative alliance based on equality and solidarity to pool resources, skills, and expertise for the common good.

Programmatic challenges

Program management practices should be developed for malaria control efforts that will help various groups of operators at different levels of the health system to implement tasks in a coordinated manner. Traditionally, malaria control activities have been undertaken under the auspices of a national malaria control program through a vertical system, with little input from the general health services and from other sectors. Although this may work in certain situations for a limited time, any narrowly defined program is inherently unsustainable

Intersectoral partnerships promote the implementation of packages of interventions

Such specialized programs must eventually be incorporated into the general health system.

Several effective interventions can be delivered through other health programs, including those that pertain to reproductive and child health. Intermittent preventive treatment, for example, can be provided to pregnant women as part of antenatal services in endemic areas. To ensure a satisfactory impact on the disease burden, programs must be technically sound. National strategies should include advocacy in order to ensure adequate funding.

Malaria control also requires the participation and collaboration of various agencies devoted to agriculture, tourism, finance, education, urban or rural development, and meteorological services, as well as the private sector and NGOs. Intersectoral partnerships at national levels promote a concerted effort toward the implementation of selected packages of interventions. A national strategic plan should be developed that coordinates the efforts of all stakeholders within a multiyear implementation plan and an agreed set of milestones and outcomes.

Traditionally, malaria control has depended on earmarked resources and budget lines. The commitment of the finance ministry appears to be essential, as it allocates funds to different sectors, including health. National-scale interventions, however, require comprehensive decisionmaking at various levels of the general health system to allocate appropriate resources. In particular, district health managers should have enough resources for their malaria-related activities. Quality management and decisionmaking needs must be met at the district level.

Successful malaria interventions can bring economic gains. One route to economic development can accrue from close links between the agriculture and malaria control sectors. The greatest contemporary burden of malaria in Sub-Saharan Africa is shouldered by people engaged in subsistence agriculture. It may be that rural poverty and subsistence agriculture are fostered by malaria and vice versa. Breaking out of this cycle will require conversion to cash crops and a simultaneous investment in malaria control efforts. Economically productive agriculture provides a payoff to governments through taxation. It is also linked to export businesses, which in turn provides a motivation for ministers of finance to invest in malaria control.

Encouraging export trade operating through urban centers, many of which are linked to profitable businesses in more rural areas, introduces a demand for malaria control in both areas to minimize days of work lost due to the disease. Enhanced labor productivity and increased company profits benefit governments through tax revenues. Reduced risk of malaria may facilitate development, and this can induce cycles of health and wealth that provide incentives to governments to the point where investment in health initiatives becomes a clear priority. Fostering economic development through simultaneous reduction of malaria risk in rural as well as urban areas has an interesting but limited history (Watson 1921). Much opportunity remains for expanding on such development. The involvement of the private sector in malaria control efforts will contribute largely to program sustainability by encouraging local procure ment of program support.

Chapter 7

Developing a global plan to achieve the Millennium Development Goal target for malaria

Development of a global plan for malaria control is a prerequisite for coordinated resource mobilization, sustained implementation, and monitoring efforts to achieve the Millennium Development Goal target for malaria.

Conditions for achieving a sustained impact

The conditions required for achieving a sustained reduction in the burden imposed by malaria include the following:

- The necessary political commitment must be made.
- The necessary human and financial resources must be available.
- An appropriate disease control strategy, including monitoring and evaluation mechanisms, must be formulated.
- Appropriate malaria control programs must be designed and planned as part of country-specific poverty reduction strategies.
- Control activities must be integrated into the activities of district- and national-level healthcare delivery services, linking the ministries of health, related governmental agencies, the donor community, NGOs, civil society organizations, the private sector, and the UN agencies. The resulting partnerships would conduct control efforts under government ownership and leadership.
- The donor community and the UN agencies must be committed to providing technical guidance and mobilizing resources.
- The necessary commodities should be readily available and these commodities should be provided free to the end users in malaria-endemic countries. It is, however, essential to develop and implement, over the long term, a financing scheme for malaria control that eliminates dependence on external donors and is self-sustaining for the countries themselves.

> **Any effort to reduce the burden of malaria must rest on accurate estimates of the current burden**

- Quality and effectiveness of antimalarial commodities must be ensured and regularly monitored.

The process of realizing these conditions needs to start with identifying districts within countries, where time-series data of defensible malaria prevalence rates are available and where an effective data collection and monitoring system is in place. Most national malaria control programs lack necessary human or financial resources to effectively monitor malaria-related morbidity and mortality and the progress of program implementation.

A practical approach to this problem is to begin with available resources and proceed incrementally as the program develops. However, it is important that malaria-endemic countries be supported by development partners and international agencies, which often develop their own monitoring systems and work independently, in their efforts to establish a health information system at the district and national levels.

Developing a global plan for reducing the burden of malaria

Any effort to reduce the burden of malaria must rest on accurate estimates of the current burden, both in place and in time. These would have to include information about local ecosystems that would help to specify the intervention packages that are tuned to the district- and village-level situations. This would provide a basis for prioritizing districts within countries where systemic health system enhancement should be initiated and where malaria control would clearly be an important part of the local programs.

The information base created in this process would include cost estimates for malaria and also for effectively implementing systemic district-level health systems. Locally relevant objectives for the reduction of the malaria burden could meaningfully be specified with this information. Gaps in district-level funding that are not currently being filled by funds allocated from national governments would be identified. Thus there would be clear knowledge of the magnitude and geographical distribution of needed short-term funds from the donor community. The information-gathering process would also provide the basis for a global business plan for relieving the burden of malaria.

The process for developing a global business plan is similar to the process for national plans. However, country plans would be more comprehensive and detailed about costing activities, deployment of personnel, the quantity of antimalarial commodities required, the extent of the population to be protected, and strategies for supervising, monitoring, and assessing impact and for scheduling timelines for implementation. National governments would be responsible for setting priorities on sequencing districts during systemic health systems improvements, thereby explicitly defining a scaling-up process at the level of district health systems. For those districts where the burden of malaria is high, malaria control would be embedded within the district-level health system. Accompanying monitoring and surveillance technology would be

A realistic and regular assessment of the malaria burden requires an understanding of the dynamics of malaria transmission

introduced, or improved as the case may be, so that it is an integral part of the scaling-up process.

The following actions are required for developing antimalarial implementation plans:

- Assess the malaria burden.
- Assess the status of malaria control and scaling-up.
- Identify and prioritize problems.
- Establish linkages with existing health systems.
- Establish linkages with economic development and poverty reduction efforts and develop effective partnership strategies.
- Develop effective commodity management systems.
- Develop effective monitoring and evaluation systems.
- Develop effective advocacy strategies.
- Conduct targeted operational research to address strategically important questions.
- Undertake a systematic needs assessment to determine cost and financing requirements.

Components of a global plan

The components of a global plan to address the malaria burden are assessment, evaluation of current programs, linking to the development of health systems and human resources, economic development and poverty reduction efforts, commodity management, renewal of current interventions and products, monitoring and evaluation, advocacy, and specific operational research. Each of the identified components is described below.

Assessment of the global malaria burden

A realistic and regular assessment of the malaria burden requires an understanding of the dynamics of malaria transmission and of identifying factors that affect trends in malaria incidence and mortality. Such a calculation would include estimates of the effects of any interventions that may be occurring. This would reflect the nature of the strategy that guides the intervention, the availability of essential commodities, human resources capacity, the adequacy of financial resources, the quality of healthcare delivery, logistical issues, political stability, and the quality of service provided by the national malaria programs. The actual global malaria burden is not well understood, particularly in Africa, because the health information systems there are so rudimentary. As a result, the annual global malaria-attributed mortality estimates vary from 700,000 deaths to 2.7 million, 90 percent of them in Africa (WHO 2000c).

WHO and UNICEF have assessed the status of various antimalarial activities and presented these results in the form of the *Africa Malaria Report 2003*. Country-specific control efforts and the extent of the malaria burden on health services was the main thrust of this assessment.

An important part of the global malaria plan is building stronger national health systems

Evaluation of current malaria control programs

The following components require attention when evaluating the status of an antimalarial program: efficacy of program organization, extent of managerial capacity, availability of resources, relevance of activities being conducted, adaptation to local epidemiological situations, adequacy of diagnostic and treatment practices, extent of coverage, and quality of service. The effectiveness of antimalarial programs depends critically on realistic resource allocation.

The package of effective antimalarial interventions includes methods for improved diagnosis and treatment, intermittent preventive treatment during pregnancy, distribution of insecticide-treated nets, application of indoor residual spraying, and source reduction by environmental management and larvicidal measures. The impact of the package depends on the level of coverage and also on the optimal selection of combinations of interventions in accordance with local ecological and epidemiological conditions. Although in the short term the health sector faces severe absorptive capacity constraints in most developing countries, adequate funding and good planning will make it feasible to scale up from current low coverage levels to more than 80 percent in about three to four years.

Good planning is required at national and district levels; it is contingent on local situation analyses, and should include material on information systems, training, human resource management, communication, community mobilization, demand creation, and quality assurance. A crucial component, too often neglected, is logistics and supply chain management. In many countries, large quantities of nets, insecticides, artemisinin-based medicines, and rapid diagnostic tests will need to be managed, and the existing infrastructure may need to be upgraded for these exigencies.

Malaria epidemics and complex emergencies can greatly increase costs of operation and jeopardize impact. Experience has shown that it is important to maintain emergency funds and revolving emergency stocks. It is essential in reporting on coverage and impact not to neglect those people who are most affected by such emergencies, as they currently account for a large proportion of the world's malaria burden. A specific line of products for malaria control in complex emergencies is under development by industry in cooperation with WHO and NGOs.

A thorough assessment of the malaria situation and the status of control efforts should be the basis for assessing and reorienting current malaria control strategies as well as their implementation and management approaches.

Linking malaria control with the development of health systems and human resources

An important part of this global plan is building stronger national health systems as a platform for delivering essential antimalarial commodities and effective interventions to those at risk of malaria, especially in the poorest segments of endemic populations.

The sustainable development of human resources presents the most formidable challenge of all

Human resource development. The efficacy of antimalarial interventions depends largely on human resources devoted to the effort. The human resource development plan should comprise the following:

- Central-level institutional development for managing human and financial resources as well as capacity for partnership with private, commercial sector, economic development projects; subcontracting; and information management. Cross-program links, especially with HIV/AIDS, tuberculosis, and maternal and child health, are also important.
- Capacity development for microplanning at district level and for establishing cross-program links with other health programs whenever feasible.
- Development of community-based services for prevention and treatment.

In view of the general attrition of the public health workforce in many developing countries, the sustainable development of human resources presents the most formidable challenge of all. Although training and supervision are necessary elements, and should be addressed at a global level by developing standardized training materials and tools, it will be necessary to take bold measures to maintain staff, probably by intervening to ensure attractive employment conditions through such measures as salary supplements. Such measures could be associated with a high risk of graft, wage inflation, and stimulation of rent-seeking. Unless they are planned in a broad health system framework, these measures could rapidly deplete those branches of the health system that are not benefiting from substantial donor support. "Ground rules" for international financial support should be established.

Service delivery. Continuous high-coverage service delivery depends on human resources, logistics, communication, infrastructure, program coordination, quality control, and supervision. These elements may appear simple, but they are critical for the success of any program and precise planning is required to ensure allocation of necessary resources, which are often underestimated. One of the important problematic coordination issues concerns the frequently conflicting demands for maintaining fixed routine services and outreach campaigns. Such problems occur frequently in the context of polio and measles campaigns, and in many countries health services are learning to deal with them.

Linking malaria control with economic development and poverty reduction efforts

In parallel with initiating improvements and developing systemic district-level health systems, with support from the international donor community, it is essential to lay the groundwork for the takeover of financing by national governments themselves. Two immediate steps toward independence from the donor community can be:

Such revenue management plans are at the core of a mechanism for ensuring sustainability

- Initiate a process of transformation from subsistence farming to cash crops.
- Heavily promote foreign direct investment in endemic countries, accompanied by within-country legislation that targets a small fraction of the increased income to the health sector.

The first point would build strong linkages between the agriculture and health sectors, as substantial at-risk populations for malaria currently engage in subsistence farming (De Plaen, Seka, and Koutoua 2004; Girardin and others 2004; Mutero and others 2004; Sissoko and others 2004). The transformation could, in the short term, be partly financed by joint agriculture-health donor coalitions. However, as local wealth increases with financial benefit also accruing to the government, a fresh incentive is provided for support from both the finance and agriculture ministries favoring allocation of resources to support district-level health systems.

The second point requires demonstration of successful examples to be followed by malaria-endemic countries. One obvious beginning is in the oil producing countries of Africa. With increased political will and assistance from organizations such as Transparency International,[1] of the publicly stated revenues that the governments receive from oil, a fraction, (say, 1.5–3 per cent) could be allocated to the health sector. These would suffice to finance antiretroviral treatment for AIDS patients who need it, malaria control, and more broadly, improvement—and even development from scratch—of district level health services. More generally, legislation within countries indicates that public health action plans that are an outgrowth of health impact assessment for development projects should be financed with a fraction of the revenues that accrue to the government from these initiatives. However, such oil-producing and precious stone–mining malaria-endemic countries will require technical and legal support from the developed world to ensure that they receive a fair share of the wealth that will be generated.

Development of such revenue management plans is currently in its infancy; but it is the core mechanism for ensuring sustainability of district and national-level health systems and breaking dependence on the donor community. Development projects—and their lenders—should evaluate potential health impacts and integrate them into decisionmaking processes and agreements such as the Equator Principles.[2]

These are but a few of the immediate possibilities that need to be pursued in parallel with the short-term donor financing discussed previously. A limited set of industries is already engaged in open dialogue on these issues with governments, banks, and tropical health experts. Cross-talk among these groups needs strong encouragement and support, as there is very little history to date of dialogue between the health, business, government, and financial communities that would lead to symbiotic improvements in the health of people in endemic countries, with correlating improvements in business activity.

Insecticides and antimalarial medicines must be administered in combinations

Commodity management

The core interventions depend on sufficient supplies of quality products, many of which are just becoming available, such as fixed-dose combinations of artemisinin-based combination therapies (ACTs), rapid diagnostic tests, and long-lasting insecticidal nets. It is desirable to strengthen the capacity of health ministries to develop and manage procurement and distribution systems for all health-related supplies and commodities. However, given the immature markets for some products, the rapidly increasing demands, and the risk of substandard and counterfeit products, a certain degree of international support will be required. The actions required are:

- Forecast needs and demand in the short, medium and long term.
- Communicate forecasts to producers.
- Cooperate with and among producers to improve quality.
- Support "soft contracts" with financial guarantees for producers of products requiring considerable lead time (such as ACTs).
- Procure commodities in bulk (especially for clusters of small countries with similar needs).
- Prequalify products based on specifications, documentation, and inspection of production sites.
- Control the quality of products at importation and at end-use points.
- Combat fake and counterfeit products through international cooperation, law enforcement, and mobilization of civil society.

Administering the ACTs will require a global subsidy "upstream" that will reduce costs by facilitating the production and distribution chain. The ACTs should become available at a cost similar to that of chloroquine to end-users in endemic countries (Institute of Medicine 2004). Rapid diagnostic capacity will require similar subsidies.

Renewing interventions and the products on which they are based

The eventual blunting of any biocide used continually on a large scale is perhaps inevitable because of the evolution of the vector, both physiologically and behaviorally. Even vaccines may eventually lose efficacy against malaria parasites. In order to reduce the likelihood of such evolution, insecticides and antimalarial medicines must be administered in combinations. Although the ACT strategy may, indeed, delay the onset of resistance, combinations inevitably expose the pathogen or vector population to more substances at the same time. Under certain circumstances, this may expend an array of resources over a shorter time than if they were exposed sequentially. The use of biocides, therefore, is probably time-limited. Unless an endless chain of independently acting insecticides, medicines, or vaccines is available, their intensive use tends to prejudice their continued application. The alternative is to devise programs that permit de-intensification after certain reasonable goals are met (Spielman, Kitron, and Pollack 1993).

Good targeting (often referred to as *judicious use* in vector control) will reduce the quantity of biocide used, thereby reducing selection pressure on the pathogen or vector population. Such a measure, however, will help delay resistance only if a large reservoir of the targeted organism is not exposed. For antimalarial medicines, those with a short half-life (such as quinine and the artemisinin derivatives) are less likely to induce resistance than those with a long half-life, an observation that lies at the heart of the extensive use of ACTs. If the use of biocides is to be scaled-up, program sustainability requires many new biocides in the pipeline that will replace those that have been blunted.

One urgent research need is to identify new antimalarial medicines that are safe enough to be used for intermittent preventive treatment during pregnancy (and possibly in infancy), when SP is no longer effective because of resistance. Although the most dramatic setbacks in malaria control have been caused by the development of resistance to antimalarial medicines, there is now room for optimism because of the promising number of new antimalarials in the pipeline. In contrast, great uncertainty surrounds the use of insecticides. Consultation among industry, scientists, and other partners is urgently needed to stimulate the development of new products. New methods such as vaccines and genetically modified mosquitoes should also be included in the strategic framework, provided that they work.

Much room remains for the improvement of existing antimalarial tools and interventions. Industry and academic laboratories are already working on novel long-lasting net treatment techniques that could be used in the field and would be inexpensive. There is a need for improved rapid diagnostic tests, especially with increased diagnostic sensitivity. Some of the ACTs currently in use, such as artesunate plus amodiaquine, need to be developed as fixed-dose combinations that would fulfill regulatory standards. This is also the case for artemisinin-derivative suppositories, which are potentially extremely useful for treatment of severe malaria at the community level.

Monitoring and evaluation

For the development of a global plan, concrete details about what indicator will be reported when and by whom must be added so that it is clear to all stakeholders how progress toward goals, objectives, and targets will be gauged year by year and country by country.

Advocacy

A global plan must be accompanied by an advocacy plan. The main purpose of an advocacy plan is to present goals and targets and estimated costs, as well as the dimensions of the malaria problem and the collateral effects of the plan. It would be important to stress the need for a strong argument for sustained and substantial donor support and to obtain firm commitments.

Any operational research agenda needs to be updated frequently in response to emerging problems and new opportunities

Operational research to address strategically important questions

A number of problematic malaria-related issues require research attention. Any operational research agenda needs to be updated frequently in response to emerging problems and new opportunities, especially those related to applying new tools. The most important issues in operational research are:

- Using rapid diagnostic tests in low transmission areas.
- Ensuring the safety and efficacy of ACTs at the community level.
- Improving distribution and maintenance of insecticide-treated nets, including collaborating with agencies dealing with immunization, reproductive health, and community-based programs.
- Assessing the role of environmental management for larval control.
- Developing strategies for urban malaria control.
- Developing systems for epidemic forecasting and prevention.
- Adapting GIS, GPS, and remote sensing for malaria control.
- Identifying the characteristics of houses that might mitigate the risk of malaria infection.
- Identifying characteristics of agricultural practice that affect the intensity of malaria transmission.

Needs assessment: costing and financing

If coverage rates and benchmarks are agreed upon and populations at risk at the district and community levels are well defined, the calculation of the total cost of a program is relatively straightforward. These costs, however, will not remain constant, and the following trends and issues should be considered:

- Increasing urbanization will tend to decrease malaria morbidity and mortality.
- The increasing HIV/AIDS burden may tend to increase the impact of malaria on communities, especially on urban populations with relatively low immunity.
- Costs of commodities, especially antimalarial medicines (such as ACTs) are expected to decrease within a few years, from about $2.50 per adult dose to approximately $1.20 per adult dose or less. Although synthetic endoperoxides may decrease the cost of ACT-like combinations, the possibility should be entertained that future antimalarial medicines could be even more expensive.
- Decreased malaria incidence will translate into decreased malaria hospitalizations and may considerably decrease the consumption of antimalarial medicines, if specific diagnosis proves reliable and feasible and is widely adopted and accepted as a prerequisite to antimalarial treatment. Under all circumstances, the feasibility of using rapid diagnostic tests for diagnosis will be decisive for treatment costs. The research evidence for this diagnostic tool is not yet available, and it is therefore necessary to consider scenarios with and without rapid diagnostic tests in costing exercises.

There is broad international consensus that effective malaria control interventions must be scaled up rapidly to achieve impact

- Although most commodity costs for novel products tend to go dow with time, the need for replacement—as resistance develops—wi mean that prices will increase once again. One of the main purposes c international cooperation is to dampen such fluctuations.
- In the current phase, there is broad international consensus that effe tive malaria control interventions must be scaled up rapidly to achiev impact. Although external financing will be the main source of fundir for antimalarial activities, at least through 2015, this responsibility mu ultimately devolve on national governments.

On the basis of costing of all activities in research projects, the costs c achieving 70 percent coverage of children under five with insecticide-treate nets (using deltamethrin), implementing intermittent preventive treatment fc first pregnancies, and changing first-line treatment to and scaling up ACT i Sub-Saharan Africa has been estimated at $824 million in 2003 U.S. dolla (Mills and Shillcutt 2004a) (table 7.1). The cost estimate for each interventic would probably be supported by most experienced malaria control planners. Fc instance, the annualized cost estimate of insecticide-treated nets compares wit another published estimate, which found that providing nets free of charge t all of rural Africa would cost $295 million per year (Curtis and others 2003).

There is room for improvement, especially for scenarios with and without rap diagnostic tests and for the control of epidemics and complex emergencies, as we as the use of indoor residual spraying and larval control in specific situations. In global plan, it will have to be estimated how the expenditures should be allocate between the GFATM, other donors, and governments; probably some increase governmental investments over time will be required. According to the propos from the Institute of Medicine, ACTs should basically be subsidized "upstream Subsidization from sources such as the GFATM in the short run must be replace by national government support as part of sustainable economic development.

For malaria-endemic countries outside Africa, estimating cost will be mo difficult because of the difficulty in estimating the populations that need to be pr tected by particular vector control measures. Furthermore, in many of these cou tries, the national malaria control budget is already substantial and it is importa to avoid simply replacing government funding with international funding.

Table 7.1

Costs of a package of malaria control interventions in Sub-Saharan Africa

2003 U.S. dollars

a. Includes cost of providing bednets for all family members to maximize mosquito mortality.

Source: Mills and Shillcutt 2004a.

Intervention	Annualized per capita cost	Total annualized cost (millions)
Insecticide-treated bednets	8.12 per child[a]	496
Intermittent preventive treatment	2.02 per pregnancy	10
Changing to ACT	0.83 per malaria case	140
Scaling up ACT	5.66 per malaria case	177
Total		824

Resource mobilization: needs assessment at the global level

WHO has commissioned a study of the global cost of malaria in support of the UN Millennium Project Working Group on Malaria. Costs were estimated for an accelerated global scale-up of a set of standard antimalarial interventions between 2005 and 2015. A full costing for programs of standard antimalarial interventions was developed for 70 malarious countries that satisfied minimum criteria on relative degree of population exposure to malaria and economic need. The individual population growth rate for each country is used to anticipate each country's growing needs. The primary scenario estimates the cost of the minimum set of interventions necessary to achieve both the 2010 Abuja targets and the Millennium Development Goals for malaria by 2015. The total global cost is estimated at $31.9 billion, corresponding to about $3 billion per year.

Specific interventions or capacity-building activities included as assumptions in the costing are:

- Provide long-lasting insecticidal nets free to high-risk population groups, and replace them after four years of use.
- Introduce ACTs in all areas with significant *P. falciparum* transmission, and rapid diagnostic tests where malaria transmission is less intense and many fevers derive from causes other than malaria.
- Provide SP-based intermittent preventive treatment to all pregnant women where malaria transmission is stable.
- Ensure the availability of adequate supplies of specific therapies and general clinical support to treat cases of severe and complicated malaria.
- Improve epidemic prevention and response capabilities, including enhanced surveillance systems and application of indoor residual spraying where malaria transmission is unstable.
- Support particular elements of the health infrastructure that are critical for the efficient implementation of scaled-up antimalarial efforts (including transportation and laboratory equipment).
- Train community health workers and existing health facility staff in prevention measures, new treatment protocols, and diagnostics.
- Produce and distribute community-directed strategic communications that reinforce knowledge of malaria prevention, early recognition of symptoms, and the need to seek treatment promptly.
- Reduce critical gaps in human resources, including health professionals, epidemiologists, entomologists, and workers in other relevant technical fields.

Application of indoor residual spraying in stable malaria transmission areas was not explicitly estimated, but it was assumed to be interchangeable with long-lasting insecticidal net programs with similar costs. Some countries may opt for indoor residual spraying due to specific technical, operational, or cultural issues.

Intervention costs should decrease progressively because the capital costs and number of malaria cases will decrease over time

Environmental management and integrated vector management activi ties were not specifically costed because of their great diversity and lack of standardization. These activities, nevertheless, remain important, particularly because of their potential for sustainability and long-term cost effectiveness.

Generally, official WHO documents were used to obtain the costs of spe cific drugs, insecticides, and other interventions. These sources include sources and prices of selected products for the prevention, diagnosis and treatment of malaria. To simplify analysis, specific drugs (such as Coartem®) and insect cides (alpha-cypermethrin) that were neither the most nor the least expensive options were selected. In Ethiopia, as indicated in the needs assessment for malaria, DDT is the choice of insecticide for use in indoor residual spraying operations. Distribution costs were chosen from values between the maximum and minimum values estimated by various sources. In certain cases, these distribution costs were aggregated with commodity costs to ease calculation. Training and information, education, and communication costs were derived from typical programs described in successful GFATM proposals.[3] Average prices for vehicles and laboratory equipment were also derived from the item ized budgets of several GFATM proposals. Certain costs, such as the cost of funding the initial education of medical doctors, were derived independently considering the likely mixture of local and international medical schools that would be utilized. It is highly likely that particular intervention choices and local conditions within particular countries will alter the estimates derived in this analysis.

Resource mobilization: needs assessment at the country level— Ethiopia

A preliminary needs assessment for nationwide scaled-up malaria control activities in Ethiopia between 2005 and 2015 is presented in appendix 1 as an example for endemic country needs. This assessment indicates that the total cost of an integrated package of interventions implemented during this period is about $2.6 billion in Ethiopia. Although the initial cost of the intervention package is estimated to be large, intervention costs should decrease progres sively because the capital costs and number of malaria cases will decrease over time. The annual per capita costs are estimated to decrease from $6.20 to $2.40 between 2005 and 2010 and from $2.40 to $0.84 between 2010 and 2015.

The package of requirements for attaining the Millennium Development Goal target on malaria in Ethiopia includes:

- Providing rapid diagnostic tests in low-transmission areas.
- Providing equipment and reagents necessary for laboratory diagnosis.
- Adequately treating simple and complicated malaria.
- Providing optimum management of severe malaria.
- Providing intermittent preventive treatment for pregnant women who reside where transmission is intense.

Cost estimates included in malaria control programs should be based on a flexible financing plan as well as an exit strategy from dependence on external donors

- Providing long-lasting insecticide-treated nets.
- Using indoor residual spraying in epidemic-prone areas or situations, using DDT as the insecticide of choice.
- Reducing vector sources by chemical, biological, or environmental methods.
- Providing epidemic prevention and control.
- Advocating for information, education, and communication.
- Providing resources for developing guidelines on various aspects of anti-malarial intervention.
- Conducting effective monitoring and evaluation.
- Developing human resources at all levels.
- Strengthening institutions.
- Retaining health workers through incentives such as paying supplemental salaries on a par with those in the private sector.
- Undertaking operational research activities.

Recently, it was estimated that between $1.6 and $3.4 billion per year would be needed to treat all febrile cases in Africa with Coartem®, unless the current practice of treating all febrile cases is changed by introducing diagnostic tests and an improved clinical algorithm (Snow, Eckert, and Teklehaimanot 2003).

Cost estimates included in malaria control programs should be based on a flexible financing plan that continues through the year 2015 as well as an exit strategy that will relieve dependence on external donors in the longer term. Currently, the dominant malaria control donor is the GFATM. However, it is uncertain whether the GFATM has mechanisms that are best adapted to meet the recommendations from the Institute of Medicine for upstream financing of ACTs. Indeed, certain signs already suggest that GFATM mechanisms may not be ideal for securing external technical cooperation for short-term implementation, monitoring, and evaluation, or for health system research and development. The GFATM, for example, should not finance upstream research for the development of new products.

Chapter 8

Monitoring and evaluation

It is becoming increasingly important for countries to measure the progre
and evaluate the impact of their malaria control programs accurately. Mon
toring and evaluation systems are generally established after program obje
tives, strategies, and activities have been defined. These systems, which inclu
a number of key indicators and measurable targets, allow program manage
and partners to monitor the implementation of planned activities in terms
input, output, and outcome within a coherent framework.

An effective monitoring and evaluation system can capture data in a
organized and cost-effective way and will contribute to more efficient alloc
tion of resources for disease-specific activities. Therefore it is important th
monitoring and evaluation be integrated in an overall evidence-based plannir
system at district, regional, and national levels. Such a systemic approach
critical in view of the fact that existing health information systems (HIS) a
weak and inadequate in most countries. This is largely because monitorir
and evaluation are not considered integral parts of evidence-based decisio
making. Often data and information (the product of analysis) are availab
to decisionmakers. However, necessary actions (such as policy changes ar
timely adoption and adaptation of interventions) are not taken readily becau
of communication and follow-up problems. This chapter outlines the key cor
cepts and main approaches to data collection for monitoring and evaluatir
malaria control at district, national, and global levels.

Monitoring and evaluation of health programs

Monitoring is the routine tracking of the performance of various program cor
ponents (WHO and RBM 2004). Program managers depend on the resultir
parameters to determine which areas require greater effort and may contribu
to an improved response. They also rely on periodic retrospective evaluatic

Monitoring and evaluation help program managers allocate resources, assess performance, and demonstrate impact

to allocate resources and modify program direction. In a well designed monitoring and evaluation system, monitoring contributes greatly toward evaluation. The choice of indicators for monitoring will depend on the reporting level within the health system. At the global level, monitoring focuses mainly on outcome indicators to monitor trends in intervention coverage. At the country level, monitoring is used to track progress of planned interventions, resource allocation, and possible adjustment of program activities, as well as to measure outcome and impact.

Evaluation is the episodic assessment of the change in targeted results that can be attributed to interventions (WHO and RBM 2004). In other words, evaluation attempts to link a particular output or outcome directly to a particular intervention or a package of interventions following a period of implementation. Evaluation helps program managers determine the value or worth of a particular program.

Malaria-related Millennium Development Goal, targets, and indicators

Goal 6, "Combat HIV/AIDS, malaria, and other diseases," includes malaria-specific targets and indicators (box 8.1). In most countries, the data available for indicators 21a and 21b will be the number of malaria cases and deaths reported monthly and annually with or without confirmed diagnosis as part of the routine HIS. Clinical malaria and confirmed cases from outpatient departments can provide information for measuring morbidity rates. Likewise, the proportion of malaria inpatients could be used as a proxy for measuring the incidence of severe malaria. Malaria-specific mortality rates can also be derived from hospital deaths. However, given the low coverage of health services, it is evident that the data obtained from the routine HIS will underestimate the malaria disease burden. The majority of the rural populations do not have access to formal health services.

Although malaria is a global health problem, it is estimated that 90 percent of malaria deaths in the world today occur in Africa south of the Sahara, and 90 percent of those deaths are among children less than five years old (WHO 2000c). The key objective of malaria control efforts in Africa is, therefore, to reduce mortality from malaria in young children. In addition to Goal 6, the focus on reducing malaria-related deaths among young children in Africa links the disease directly to Goal 4, "Reduce child mortality." It is unlikely that Goal 4 can be met without substantial reductions in childhood deaths due to malaria in most African countries. Besides children, pregnant women are particularly vulnerable to malaria. Use of effective preventive measures (such as the administration of intermittent preventive treatment and the use of insecticide-treated nets) to reduce maternal mortality and morbidity and improve well-being during pregnancy links malaria to Goal 5 "Improve maternal health." It is also important to consider people who live in unstable transmission areas, particularly

Box 8.1

**Goal 6: Combat
HIV/AIDS, malaria,
and other diseases**

Souce: UN Millennium
Project

**Target 8. Have halted by 2015 and begun to reverse the incidence of malaria and
other major diseases**

Indicators

21a. Prevalence rate associated with malaria.

21b. Malaria-related death rates in children under five and other population groups.

22a. Proportion of children under five and other population groups in malaria-risk area
using effective prevention measures (insecticide-treated nets, indoor residual spraying
and source reduction).

22b. Proportion of children under five and other population groups with malaria who ar
appropriately treated.

those prone to epidemics. As malaria is a leading cause of illness and absen
teeism in school-age children, effective malaria control will accelerate progres
on Goal 2, "Achieve universal primary education." Thus reducing the burder
of malaria directly or indirectly contributes to the achievement of Goals 2, 4, 5
and 6 and their accompanying targets. The synergies between the Millenniun
Development Goals are vital to any country's sustainable development.

Coverage measures

In addition to measuring impact, it will be important to evaluate the cov
erage rates of both prevention and treatment interventions undertaken at th
district and community levels. These interventions include household use c
insecticide-treated nets, application of indoor residual spraying in epidemic
prone areas, administration of intermittent preventive treatment to pregnar
women living in high endemic areas, and prompt and effective treatment c
febrile malaria illness in young children and other population groups.

Main approaches to data collection for monitoring malaria contro

For malaria control, disease-specific data can be obtained at two primar
levels: the health facility and health system level through routine HIS, and th
community and household level through Demographic Surveillance System
(DSS), Demographic and Health Surveys (DHS), Multiple Indicator Cluste
Surveys (MICS), and Malaria Indicator Surveys (MIS).

Health information systems

Health information systems constitute the main source of data on malari
cases and malaria-related deaths, and are particularly useful for monitorin
time trends in the disease burden at district, regional, and national levels. Mor
specifically, the routine HIS captures the following data on case managemer
and outcomes at the health facility level:

- Proportion of malaria cases seen in outpatient consultations.
- Hospital admission rate due to severe malaria.

Health information systems are particularly useful for monitoring severe disease and case fatality rates among hospital inpatients

- Malaria mortality rate in hospitals.
- Case fatality rate of malaria among hospital inpatients.
- Severe anemia admission rate in children under five years of age due to malaria.
- Reductions in the prevalence of anemia and acute malaria in pregnant women.

These routine HIS data contribute to the understanding of the dynamics of severe disease and case fatality rates among hospital inpatients where the population of interest is those who arrive at a health facility. Facility-based data are most useful in monitoring health facility needs for antimalarial medicines and other essential commodities.

In most countries, existing HIS are inadequate and are unable to provide robust data for effective monitoring and evaluation. Reporting from health facilities to districts and from districts to the ministry of health varies in its completeness and timeliness and often does not include health data from other sources, such as nongovernmental facilities. More important, most malaria patients in endemic countries either do not seek treatment or are treated outside the formal health sector. Finally, most deaths occur at home and are not captured by the routine HIS. The deaths occurring at home are recorded by vital registration systems in only a few countries, but these registration systems are usually incomplete and are not very specific. Therefore, although the routine HIS data can be potentially useful for local program planning, the use of facility-based data as a proxy for population health is based on the assumption that the population attending health services reflects the health problems of those who do not attend. This is generally not the case.

Improvements in both the quality of HIS and access to health services are required before health-facility data can be relied on for monitoring epidemiological trends. In some countries, a promising strategy to strengthen health information systems is to recruit randomly selected inpatient and outpatient formal health service providers, to act as sentinels for monitoring time trends in disease burdens. Given adequate diagnostics and human resources capacity, these sentinel health facilities can capture important data on trends in case fatality rates, disease presentation, and treatment failures. The data derived from sentinels will permit revised estimation of commodity needs at the health system level. Computer-based information systems capturing facility-based data on malaria cases have been developed in a number of endemic countries (such as South Africa); the development of computer-based systems in Africa can provide a basis for effective monitoring and management of large-scale programs.

Collecting malaria-specific data outside the routine HIS is necessary to monitor various malaria-directed activities. Indoor residual spraying application and coverage, distribution, and use of insecticide-treated nets, malaria risk mapping, studies on the efficacy of antimalarials, use of environmental management measures, studies on vector susceptibility to insecticides, and community-based

Community-based information on prevention and treatment practices is critical for monitoring program success

interventions are supervised primarily by personnel dedicated to malaria prgrams and community health workers. Such activities are monitored and evalated through specific surveys or the establishment of sentinel sites.

Community and household surveys

Community-based information on prevention and treatment practices is criticfor monitoring the progress and impact of malaria control. The greatest burdof the disease and the greatest need for prevention and control efforts tend occur in isolated rural settings where a large proportion of cases are managed home. Deaths occur outside the formal healthcare setting and are not reportin hospital statistics or national vital statistics. Therefore, the most importalevel at which to measure impact is the household level. Data can be obtainprospectively through continuous surveillance by sample registration or sentiDSS or retrospectively through periodic, national, cross-sectional household suveys such as DHS, MICS, and MIS. Such household surveys also reveal trends coverage of insecticide-treated nets and appropriate treatment for malaria.

Demographic surveillance systems. DSS sites monitor disease and deaths prspectively in large populations with full vital event registration and are updatone to four times a year. DSS integrates census and survey data longitudinalthrough total sampling or representative sampling methods and avoids the seselection bias that is embedded in routine HIS data. Continuous surveillanapproach over time also makes it possible to link georeferenced contextual daon socioeconomic, environmental, and health systems with each individual the population (De Savigny and Binka 2004).

Currently, there are 33 DSS sites in 14 countries in Africa. These DSS sithave recently formed a network, INDEPTH (http://www.indepth-networorg), to harmonize and strengthen methods, lower costs, and address questioacross multiple sites. At present, DSS communities provide the most reliabdata on time trends in malaria mortality in children under five (Korenromand others 2003). Establishing additional DSS sites in malaria-endemic arewould enhance the ability to track changes in cause-specific mortality in chdren and also in adults at a population level. The necessary data on mortaliimpact in the short term can be derived from a strategic combination of Dand nationwide household surveys (such as DHS) supporting the backbone a sectorwide or even intersectoral management information system. It shoube a top priority for each malarious country to have a number of DSS sites.

Demographic and Health Surveys. DHS are nationwide household surveys thfocus on reproductive and child health. Typically, DHS are based on interviewith between 4,000 and 12,000 women aged 15–49 years who are sampled a multiple-stage cluster design. Because the questionnaires are standardizand structured and change little between surveys, DHS results are comparab

**The most
important
level at which
to measure
impact is the
household
level**

across countries and over time. However, if DHS are to be useful for monitoring progress and evaluating the impact of malaria control measures, they should be implemented more frequently.

Since 1998 specific questions on malaria prevention and treatment have been included in DHS. In 2001 these questions were grouped into a standard malaria module and added to the surveys conducted in malarious countries. Besides providing information on major outcome indicators, DHS are a primary source of information on all-cause under-five mortality rates, with their use of indirect demographic techniques such as birth histories. Recently DHS have also been used to measure the prevalence of anemia by hemoglobin measurement in children under five years of age. DHS are organized by Macro International, USA. Questionnaires and survey results are available on the Internet approximately one year after the field work is completed.[1]

Multiple Indicator Cluster Surveys. Between 1999 and 2001, MICS were conducted in 67 countries with support from the United Nations Children's Fund. MICS are nationally representative surveys, comprising on average 6,000 households, sampled through a two-stage cluster design. In 24 African countries where MICS were conducted, they included a malaria module with questions related to prevention and treatment. MICS also provide data on all-cause mortality among children under five years of age. Survey results and questionnaires are available on the Internet.[2]

Malaria Indicator Survey. Recently the Monitoring and Evaluation Reference Group of the RBM Partnership has worked with Macro International to develop a Malaria Indicator Survey (MIS), which may be used at a national or subnational level. The sample sizes are smaller than those required for DHS and MICS, since the primary use of these surveys is to monitor progress in coverage of insecticide-treated nets and effective treatment, but not all-cause child mortality. The MIS will, then, be less expensive to conduct than DHS or MICS and can be conducted at a subnational level, if needed. In addition, for operational reasons, both DHS and MICS are conducted during the dry season and, therefore, outside the peak malaria transmission season, whereas the MIS can—and should—be targeted to the peak transmission and combined with measurements of hemoglobin and parasite prevalence, where relevant. The entire MIS package (questionnaire, training manual, guidance on sampling and sampling sizes with costing, and so on) became available in 2004.

Summary of main approaches to data collection: toward an integrated data system

No single data source can supply all the data on process and impact indicators that are necessary for monitoring progress and evaluating the impact of malaria control. Although HIS is the main data system in use, it is not

An immediate
priority is to
strengthen
information
systems
for health

adequate for capturing population-based health data. Looking to the next 1
years, it has to be an immediate priority to strengthen information systems.
will also be important to develop a comprehensive data system that provide
both population-based household-level health data and detailed health facilit
information. It is highly recommended that priority be given to investing i
a reliable and comprehensive health information system. As it evolves, th
comprehensive system should include surveys such as DSS, DHS, MICS
MIS, and other appropriate special surveys. These tools together are critical fc
measuring impact at the community level and for district-level health syster
management as well as for use by international agencies, such as GFATM an
WHO. As investments for health increase over time, countries should explor
innovative ways to combine data from DSS, DHS, MICS, and MIS to enab
effective measurement of the impact of malaria and other health interventior
and to help plan for allocation of resources. Community-based surveys a
essential for documenting all-cause and cause-specific mortality and healtl
seeking process indicators, and in monitoring poverty reduction indicator
Longer term maintenance of all of these monitoring systems should becom
an integral part of the budget of health ministries, as outlined in chapter
Integrated data systems are a pressing priority for monitoring and evaluatin
malaria control programs.

Monitoring the effectiveness of antimalarials and insecticides

Although outside a strict definition of monitoring and evaluation, assessme
of parasite and vector sensitivity to medicines and insecticides is of paramour
importance in maintaining program effectiveness. For antimalarial combina
tion therapies, traditional *in vivo* assays should be supplemented with *in vit*
and molecular marker studies for early warning of the emergence of resistanc
Assessments of quality assurance at procurement and at the point of delivei
should also be a part of the surveillance system. Strengthening research cente
in Africa is essential to build up capacity for undertaking operational researc
and to ensure appropriate laboratory and statistical backup (such as vecto
species identification and infection rates), with a view toward developing a
appropriate skills base for monitoring and evaluation.

Developing geographic information systems and remote sensing

Establishing a national GIS platform for assessing malaria risk will require
national effort to define a high-resolution population distribution map base
on the most recent national census that will be linked to modeled distributioi
of malaria risk. In addition, GIS surfaces will be developed for transport ne
works and health service providers to enhance planning of service provisioi
All subsequent data collection will use the combined risk-population-servi
GIS platform as a sampling frame and analytical tool (for example, coveraç
versus poverty mapping).

An itemized costing system should give all unit costs and quantities explicitly

An important first step in this direction is the monitoring system developed by WHO and UNICEF based on a comprehensive GIS system, Health-Mapper. National malaria control programs are now using this system:

- To identify populations at risk.
- To assess access of communities to health care.
- To target and monitor implementation of interventions, including use of insecticide-treated nets and larvicides.
- To monitor resistance to first-line medicines.
- To integrate environmental data (such as rainfall amounts and their variability) to serve as an early warning system for epidemics.
- To assess the impact of irrigation and other environmental factors on transmission.

An important additional step is the recently launched online WHO global atlas of infectious diseases. A new tool for infectious disease surveillance and control, it builds upon the features of HealthMapper. More than 300 indicators for more than 20 infectious diseases are included in this database.

Routine remote sensing and modeling can be used in both a prospective and a retrospective manner to facilitate malaria control efforts in forecasting and preventing epidemics. Currently, an experiment is under way that combines remote sensing data with real-time health facility data to validate the relevance of remote sensing (Cox and others 1999). Integrated with other data sources, remote sensing is a potentially useful tool for national malaria control programs and district-level health planners. Their development depends on the availability of human and technical resources.

These GIS and remote sensing technologies are meant to strengthen surveillance and management systems of malaria control programs. While allocating resources, care should be taken to ensure that community-based disease prevention and management activities are not reduced in favor of these technologies.

Cost-effectiveness of service provision

An itemized costing system should be developed in which all unit costs and quantities are given explicitly. These routine cost analyses can provide a framework for an ongoing assessment of changes in unit costs (such as the price of insecticide-treated nets or antimalarials) or quantities (such as the number of insecticide-treated nets delivered). The data on coverage, individual effectiveness, community effectiveness, and costs can form the empirical basis for a cost-effectiveness analysis of alternative intervention strategies and should be embedded within the national GIS platform of risk, changing disease burden, and service access.

Linkage of malaria monitoring with poverty alleviation

As part of the GIS platform, poverty mapping should accompany malaria-risk mapping. This would include spatial representations of the local living standards, the sources of income generation, and the distribution of wealth. Spatial association analyses will connect malaria risk to the economic status of communities as well as the neighboring centers with which they interact. The reciprocal connections between malaria control and poverty will be an integral part of these efforts. Mapping actual or potential development sites, including those of tourism and industrial areas, is expected to have a direct impact on poverty by enabling the creation of new jobs.

Malaria control programs should be planned and implemented as part of the poverty reduction strategies of endemic countries.

Chapter 9

Research and development to meet current and future needs

An extensive program of applied and basic research should be implemented to improve existing antimalarial tools and interventions.

Antimalarial medicine development

The prospects of antimalarial medicine treatment looked bleak in the past few decades. Resistance against available medicines had spread rapidly, effective treatments had diminished, and only a few new antimalarial medicines were in the development pipeline. Recently, however, the situation has improved considerably. Medicine development efforts have been invigorated by the establishment of the Medicines for Malaria Venture (MMV) along with WHO's Special Programme for Research and Training in Tropical Diseases and Walter Reed Army Institute for Research (Institute of Medicine 2004). It is important to maintain a sufficiently large, high-quality pipeline of antimalarial compounds to ensure sustainability in medicine discovery and development. Currently, several new combination regimens and entirely new classes of medicines are under development.

There are a number of projects close to completion involving fixed-dose artemisinin-based medicines with an expected registration date of 2006–07. The goal is to develop alternative combination medicines that are more effective and less costly (box 9.1). The medicine development portfolio also includes several single-agent medicines, some of which may come on the market soon after 2010 and may ultimately be used in combination with other antimalarial medicines. High on the list of such antimalarial medicines are artemisone (a new artemisinin derivative), synthetic peroxide, pyridones, isoquine, and DB 289 (a diamidine derivative). Finally, research efforts concentrate on enhancing the formulations of existing medicines. The projects include pediatric Coartem® formulation, rectal artesunate, and artesunate intravenous formulation for severe malaria (Institute of Medicine 2004).

Box 9.1

**Artemisinin
combinations in
development**

Source: MMV 2004.

- Chlorproguanil-dapsone artesunate (Lapdap artesunate).
- Pyronaridine-artesunate.
- Piperaquine-dihydroartemisinin.
- Amodiaquine-artesunate.
- Mefloquine-artesunate.

The current pipeline of new antimalarial medicines looks promising. However, developing novel compounds into safe, effective, and affordable medicine for populations living in malaria-endemic countries requires substantial and sustained funding, particularly in view of the increasing technical challenge (MMV 2003). Many malaria experts agree on the need to replace malaria monotherapies with combination therapies to extend the useful lifetime and maintain the effectiveness of antimalarial medicines. This will almost double the time and economic cost of medicine development programs. The ultimate goal in malaria research and development is to develop an effective, safe, and affordable single-dose medicine for the treatment of *P. falciparum* malaria including medicine-resistant strains, which is also efficacious against *P. vivax* malaria. Such a medicine would likely be a combination. With sufficient resources, this very ambitious goal seems attainable.

According to the recent report published by the Institute of Medicine on the economics of antimalarial medicines, an estimated $60–$80 million per year is needed to maintain the momentum of existing development activities along with $300–500 million to subsidize the use of ACTs as first-line medicines globally (Institute of Medicine 2004). Significant cost savings are possible if researchers succeed in developing low-cost and effective antimalarial medicines as targeted. This presented case becomes more compelling economically if one factors into consideration the macroeconomic benefits from effective malaria control. Aligned with the Millennium Development Goals, the priority is to maintain a sustainable pipeline of antimalarial medicines to benefit the affected populations in malaria-endemic countries (MMV 2003).

Malaria diagnostics

The use of clinical diagnosis in highly endemic areas and the advantages and disadvantages of employing rapid diagnostic tests in different settings are discussed in chapter 4. Based on that information, future research and development directions are discussed here.

Since rapid diagnostic tests do not, as yet, yield quantitative measurement of the level of parasitemia, methods that permit quantification of parasite density must be developed. Furthermore, it will be important that such tests be able to better reflect the total parasite load, including both circulating and sequestered parasites. Making tests easier to use in the field by reducing the

Intermittent preventive treatment in infants could reduce the burden of malaria significantly

number of steps and components and developing non-blood-based tests will also be necessary. The published literature on recent rapid diagnostic test trials does not indicate possible causes of performance differences among study sites (WHO 2003a). Therefore it will be helpful to create a shared bank of reagents and to establish a common network of well equipped and geographically diverse sites where new tests can be assessed. These new rapid diagnostic tests can improve our understanding of the biology of malaria in the human host (WHO 2000a).

Aside from research on the development of improved assays, it is also necessary to study the operational feasibility and acceptability of introducing rapid diagnostic tests in isolated communities and their use by private health providers. Such studies should be multidisciplinary and include economic analysis, behavioral studies, monitoring and quality control, and measurement of outcomes.

Malaria management in young children

Lacking natural immunity to malaria, children under five years of age are among those who are most vulnerable to the worst effects of *P. falciparum* infection. Deaths and severe anemia are most frequent in this age group, particularly in African countries. Although young children can be protected substantially by chemoprophylaxis administered at weekly or fortnightly intervals, such interventions are difficult to sustain and may accelerate the onset of antimalarial medicine resistance while impairing the acquisition of natural immunity against the disease. SP and amodiaquine, which yielded satisfactory results in studies of intermittent preventive treatment in infants, will not be recommended in most African countries because of their reduced efficacy.

Conducting the first study on intermittent preventive treatment in infants (IPTi), Schellenberg and colleagues demonstrated that three therapeutic doses of SP treatment administered at 2, 3, and 9 months of age during routine childhood vaccinations under the Expanded Program on Immunization reduced the rate of clinical malaria by almost 60 percent and severe anemia by 50 percent in Tanzanian infants (Schellenberg and others 2001). A second study, also conducted in Tanzania, on presumptive treatment of infants with amodiaquine during the first year of life along with routine Expanded Program on Immunization vaccinations reported similar results (Massaga and others 2003).

These findings suggest that intermittent preventive treatment in infants could reduce the burden of malaria significantly in this age group in highly endemic areas. However, any intervention delivered through the established Expanded Program on Immunization system as part of an integrated malaria control strategy should be assessed for its impact on the efficacy of vaccines devlivered by this program. A recent review of nine published clinical studies indicated that antimalarial medicines might affect the immunological response to routinely administered childhood vaccines (Rosen and Breman 2004).

Increased research attention should be placed on the vector ecology of malaria

Additional multicenter studies on the safety and efficacy of intermittent preventive treatment in infants are needed in different epidemiological settings. Therefore, at this point, intermittent preventive treatment in infants is not recommended as an intervention strategy.

Formed to resolve pending scientific questions and implementation issues about introducing intermittent preventive treatment in infants as a routine health intervention, the IPTi Consortium—an alliance of WHO, UNICEF, and leading research centers in Africa, Europe, and the United States—will conduct five studies in Africa.[1] The IPTi Consortium aims to provide sufficient evidence by early 2006 to inform policy debate on the widespread use of this strategy (IPTi Consortium 2004).

Malaria vector

Developments in malaria vector control are highly dependent on basic and applied research.

Vector ecology

Increased research attention should be placed on the vector ecology of malaria. Specifically:

- Environmental conditions that contribute to mosquito longevity remain virtually unknown.
- The effect of malaria infection on feeding frequency remains unexplored.
- Temperature relationships are poorly understood.
- Host specificity by vector mosquitoes remains a fertile field of study.
- Mosquito survival mechanisms through interepidemic periods and signals of the onset and termination of transmission are poorly understood.
- Ongoing speciation of *A. gambiae* and its relationship to adaptation to different ecological niches needs to be understood.

Insecticide development

The arsenal of low-risk and cost-effective public health insecticides, most notably for preventing malaria, is depleted for a variety of reasons (such as insecticide resistance and lack of re-registration). The number of new insecticide products in the pipeline is also dwindling. The global market for public health pesticides has become less attractive to the industry as a result of low and unpredictable return on investment in research and development of new insecticides.

Pyrethroids are the only contact insecticides that have reached the market for vector control in the past two decades (Zaim and Guillet 2002), and they constitute the only group of insecticides currently recommended for treating mosquito nets (Zaim, Aitio, and Nakashima 2000). Pyrethroid resistance has, however, emerged in major mosquito populations in Africa and other malaria-endemic parts of the world and has been spreading rapidly (Casimir

The number of new insecticide products in the pipeline is dwindling

2003; Chandre and others 1999; Hargreaves and others 2000; Singh and others 2002). A very high frequency of the *kdr* resistance gene in *A. gambiae* in central Côte d'Ivoire does not prevent insecticide-treated bednets from working well in killing mosquitoes that enter huts, in controlling malaria, and in reducing the infective vector populations in villages. However, one should be prepared with alternatives that have been proven to be safe and effective in case more powerful forms of pyrethroid resistance emerge (such as *A. funestus* in South Africa; Hargreaves and others 2000).

Making selective and judicious use of currently available insecticides, particularly within the context of integrated vector management, and increasing the cost-effectiveness of existing tools (such as improved insecticide formulations and application technologies including long-lasting insecticidal nets) are among short- to medium-term solutions. These strategies should be supported by improved capacity for planning, implementing, and evaluating vector control activities, coupled with effective insecticide resistance monitoring and management. However, as a longer term strategy, identifying mechanisms and procedures for developing new insecticidal compounds for public health use is of high priority. Because it takes 7–10 years to bring a newly developed compound to registration, immediate action is required (WHO 2004b).

Modification of vector populations

Notable progress has recently been achieved in attempts to genetically transform anopheline mosquitoes. Genes have been incorporated into the mosquito genome that would reduce the ability of certain malaria ookinetes to develop into the sporozoite stage, thus developing mosquitoes incapable of transmitting malaria parasites (Ghosh, Moreira, and Jacobs-Lorena 2002). The three essentials of a transformation system may soon become available: competence-inhibiting genes, promoters, and driver systems. In spite of intensive efforts, however, no effector gene relevant to human malaria and no promising driver have yet been developed. Also the very difficult problem of ensuring genetic linkage of the drive system and the effector genes remains to be solved. Thus, we are still far from definite experiments designed to determine whether the malaria-competence of confined populations of vector mosquitoes can be stably and effectively reduced.

Efforts to create genetic constructs for vector anophelines should be accompanied by research programs designed to explore the circumstances under which these assets can be put into practice. It is necessary to identify test locations that are geographically isolated so that controlled releases of genetically modified mosquitoes can be conducted and their elimination made possible, if that becomes necessary. Optimum evaluation of the effectiveness of such a release can best be performed in locations where only a single vector population perpetuates infection. Ethical considerations should be defined and

An effective malaria vaccine has so far proven elusive

may include the magnitude of the release inoculum, which requires careful attention, as well as the circumstances under which a release is to take place. It is also necessary to ascertain the competence of natural vector populations in release locations and to devise models that examine the effect of a reduction in competence on the force of malaria transmission.

Malaria vaccines

Despite decades of research, an effective malaria vaccine has so far proven elusive. Natural immunity against malaria infection develops gradually after repeated infection. Yet this acquired immunity is strain-specific, requires continual boosting, and is disease modifying rather than sterilizing (Webster and Hill 2003). Some 5,300 antigens encode the *P. falciparum* parasite. We do not yet know which of these genes regulate the expression of antigens that produce the key protective immune response in human hosts and that should be targeted to develop a successful vaccine (Moorthy, Good, and Hill 2004). Each malaria infection results in the introduction of thousands of antigens into the human immune system, which differ at each stage of the parasite's life cycle (Moore, Surgey, and Cadwgan 2002). Another central issue in vaccine research, therefore, is the choice of which stage in the life cycle of the parasite to target (Richie and Saul 2002). Despite these complexities, prospects are still high, especially with the genomic sequencing of *P. falciparum* (Gardner and others 2002) and the increased research funding that has become available in recent years (Ballou and others 2004). Various candidate vaccines target different stages of parasite development:

- Pre-erythrocytic vaccines aim to avert the clinical manifestations of malaria by preventing sporozoites[2] from entering or developing within infected liver cells (Moore, Surgey, and Cadwgan 2002). The recent success of the lead vaccine candidate, RTS,S/AS02A, in a phase 2b proof-of-concept trial is very encouraging (Alonso and others 2004). The double-blind, randomized controlled trial in Mozambique involving 2,022 children ages 1–4 years revealed that the vaccine protected children against malaria attacks by 30 percent, primary infection with *P. falciparum* by 45 percent, and severe disease by 58 percent.
- Blood-stage vaccines aim to modulate the complications of malaria by preventing the invasion of red blood cells by merozoites.[3] The process of invasion is complex and rapid, involving a number of parasite proteins that are located on the surface of the merozite and that are thus transiently accessible to circulating antibodies. The most studied antigens include merozoite surface protein 1 (MSP-1, MSP2, MSP3, and apical membrane antigen 1 (Ballou and others 2004). To date, the development of such a vaccine has been hampered by antigen polymorphism (Webster and Hill 2003) and the lack of a viable target antigen or combination of antigens (Moorthy, Good, and Hill 2004).

An effective malaria vaccine should ultimately target multiple antigens and multiple stages

- Transmission-blocking (antigamete) vaccines aim to prevent vector mosquitoes from acquiring infection from an infected person, but they do not modulate the infection and confer protection to individuals. The formulation of adequately immunogenic vaccines has proven difficult, as sexual-stage antigen targets are complex proteins with precise molecular folding requirements (Ballou and others 2004). These vaccines will likely be useful for populations living in malaria-endemic areas, and there is therefore little commercial funding for their research and development (Webster and Hill 2003). The U.S. National Institute for Allergy and Infectious Disease Malaria Vaccine Development Unit has decided to clinically assess a *P. falciparum* gametocyte candidate vaccine, Pfs25 (Moorthy, Good, and Hill 2004).

It is commonly accepted that an effective malaria vaccine should ultimately target multiple antigens and multiple stages and generate humoral (antibody) and cellular immunity as well as immunological memory (Richie and Saul 2002). More research on antigenic polymorphism, duration of efficacy, means of antigen combination, and vaccine delivery systems capable of inducing the desired immune response is required. The laboratory work that is devoted to production of malaria vaccines should also be accompanied by epidemiological studies that will identify the populations to be immunized.

Chapter 10

Recommendations

The UN Millennium Project Working Group on Malaria has focused on developing and designing strategic frameworks that would ensure implementation of antimalarial interventions covering as many residents of endemic sites as possible and incorporating components tuned to local conditions. Accordingly, the working group now seeks to develop malaria control strategies based on integrated packages of interventions designed to improve health nationally while also promoting economic development locally. The components of these proposed strategies include early diagnosis of clinically apparent infection; treating with effective antimalarial medicines; using insecticide-treated bed nets; applying indoor residual spraying; appropriately managing the environment; improving housing for and extending health education to all residents of endemic sites; and improving monitoring and evaluation systems.

These interventions, if conducted with sufficient intensity and coverage and applied on a national scale, will greatly reduce morbidity and mortality and should promote economic growth. Specifically, insecticide-treated bednets should be distributed to all children in malaria-endemic areas by 2007 to achieve 100 percent coverage. Such a comprehensive strategy would promote cognitive development and school attendance. A program of basic and applied research is required that will provide a series of alternative medicines and insecticides, rapid diagnostics suitable for field use, and appropriate vaccines. The working group has identified 14 critical areas that require priority action.

1. Establish a realistic and measurable target on malaria

Because the established Millennium Development Goal target on malaria, "Have halted by 2015 and begun to reverse the incidence of malaria," is difficult to measure and interpret, the Working Group on Malaria proposes a more measurable target. The revised target is to "Reduce malaria morbidity

Ministries of health need long-term predictable commitments of funding from the international donor community

and mortality by 75 percent by 2015 from the 2005 baseline level." The proposed target and timeline are consistent with the Millennium Development Goals for improved maternal health and reduction of child mortality, because children under five years of age and pregnant women are the most vulnerable to malaria.

2. Enhance political commitment at country and global levels

Ministries of health should concentrate on their stewardship role by strengthening their planning, analytical, and public health expertise. Adequate human and financial resources should be dedicated to the pursuit of antimalarial interventions and to the development of rationales for persuading other governmental agencies to join in this effort. Ministries such as those of agriculture, trade, mines, education, and finance are likely partners in malaria control. Such intersectoral collaborations are strengthened greatly when elements of the private sector, such as philanthropic organizations and various industries (such as the oil and mining industries) are included. Endemic countries should incorporate malaria control activities into their poverty reduction strategies.

Governments should promote the use of essential antimalarial intervention tools such as medicines, insecticides, insecticide-treated nets, and indoor residual spraying. Such public goods should be available free of cost to populations at risk for malaria. These efforts will require donor community participation to mobilize resources, as malaria-endemic countries cannot afford to implement these programs on their own. At the same time, measures should be adopted that will ensure the appropriate use of financial and other resources dedicated to malaria control interventions. Requirements for transparency should be imposed on agencies that are the recipients of such resources.

3. Strengthen health systems at national and district levels

Ministries of health need long-term predictable commitments of funding from the donor community to strengthen the healthcare infrastructure in endemic countries, to provide quality laboratory services that will ensure reliable diagnosis and effective case management. Efficient mechanisms will also be required for procuring and distributing medicines, reagents, insecticides, and other essential commodities and for developing service delivery models coordinated with other health programs and effective health information and monitoring systems. These information systems would identify the most pressing health problems that can be addressed by existing technologies and also promote appropriate allocation of existing funds. Information systems for health should be modernized and strengthened and, as resources for health increase, should integrate community-level as well as facility-level data in a cohesive manner. Such comprehensive health information systems will enable planning, resource allocation, and tracking program performance through monitoring and evaluating process, outcome, and impact indicators. These

Essential antimalarial commodities should be provided free of charge to those at risk

systems are also essential for monitoring and evaluating program performance, assessing equity of health systems, and evaluating the extent to which Millennium Development Goals objectives are realized.

4. Develop human resources for program implementation

Skilled personnel are required at national and district levels to assess local situations, develop appropriate intervention strategies, guide control activities, and monitor their impact. Human resource constraints should be addressed through an appropriate combination of incentives, legislative measures, and management reforms. Motivated staff should be retained with salary supplements and hardship allowances, and housing should be provided for those working in rural areas where the malaria challenge is most pressing. Such incentives may also slow the exodus to other countries of professionals seeking better opportunities.

Training is critically required in epidemiology, entomology, laboratory diagnostics, and case management. Materials and tools that would enhance supervision, planning, and program management should be developed and produced. Existing regional malaria training centers and networks should be encouraged to produce midlevel malaria professionals knowledgeable in malaria prevention and management. These midlevel professionals should also be able to implement malaria control activities effectively and promote advocacy and community participation. Current training programs, especially in Africa, lack mechanisms to track certificate holders. Monitoring and evaluation are keys to the enhancement of the quality of work at the community level.

5. Promote social mobilization and community participation

Systems should be put in place for mobilizing communities and encouraging community participation in malaria planning and control activities. Because a large majority of the population at risk in Sub-Saharan Africa lacks access to formal health services, extension health workers, traditional birth attendants, and community health agents have a central role in the prevention and treatment of malaria. Community participation in planning and implementing malaria control efforts should be supported as an integral part of an effective district health system. The process should include establishing new health centers and health posts as part of the district health system.

6. Provide effective antimalarial supplies and commodities

Antimalarial medicines, insecticide-treated nets, and insecticides for indoor residual spraying (mainly DDT and pyrethroids) should be considered public goods and should be available free of charge to residents of endemic sites.

7. Apply an integrated package of interventions

There is no single antimalarial "magic bullet" that can bring about a sustained reduction in the malaria burden. A combined set of locally adapted

Antimalarial intervention strategies should also promote social and economic development

interventions should be used because the cycle of malaria transmission is composed of many components that vary greatly from place to place. This package of interventions includes use of insecticide-treated bednets; application of indoor residual spraying; early diagnosis of clinical infections; treatment with effective antimalarials; intermittent preventive treatment of pregnant women; management of the environment; increased health education and awareness; epidemic forecasting; early detection and control; and improved monitoring and surveillance systems and evaluation of program implementation. The Working Group on Malaria endorses the Quick Wins initiative described in the UN Millennium Project's (2005) *Investing in Development*, which recommends immediate scale-up of high impact interventions that do not require complex infrastructure to implement. Among these Quick Wins is the recommendation that insecticide-treated bednets be distributed to all children in malaria-endemic areas by 2007. Because of the tremendous potential to save lives, especially in Sub-Saharan Africa, the working group believes that the target of 100 percent insecticide-treated bednet coverage among children should be an urgent international priority. In addition, intersectoral activities such as housing improvement, agricultural modification, water resource development, and road construction should complement these malaria-directed interventions.

8. Scale up malaria control efforts to national level

At present, malaria control efforts are conducted as relatively small projects with limited coverage and scope. Because they tend to be fragmented and uncoordinated, these efforts have had little impact on the resurgence of malaria. Improving efficiency and use by expanding primary healthcare services and eliminating constraints and inadequacies are required. Control efforts should be intensified and coverage extended to include all malaria-endemic sites globally. Community-based interventions should constitute an important element in the universal strategy. Ministries of health need major donor support to scale up investments in general health systems improvement and malaria control to achieve the health-related Millennium Development Goals.

9. Promote social and economic development

Although the main objective is to reduce malaria-related mortality and morbidity, antimalarial intervention strategies should also promote social and economic development. Sustainability requires strategies designed to eliminate transmission in those sites that potentially generate wealth or that may promote social development. Wealth-generating sites include those that are devoted to tourism, mining, and manufacturing industries, as well as port facilities. Social development is promoted in schools and administrative centers.

Increased
development
assistance
is needed to
realize the
Millennium
Development
Goal target
for malaria

10. Incorporate malaria prevention and treatment approaches into school curricula

Instruction devoted to appropriate malaria-related material should be incorporated into the curricula of health-related schools (those devoted to medicine, nursing, or sanitation) as well as schools devoted to agriculture, water resources, and civil engineering. Such material should also be included in primary, secondary, and vocational schools.

11. Develop surveillance systems for early detection of malaria epidemics

The increasing trend of large-scale malaria epidemics in the world require the development of improved methods for epidemic forecasting, prevention and early detection. Development of malaria surveillance systems is crucial for epidemic preparedness and effective response in epidemic-prone areas. Multisectoral approaches reinforce effective development of early warning systems and should be supported.

12. Promote partnerships for malaria control

Existing malaria partnerships link ministries of health with representatives of UN and donor agencies but provide limited opportunity for participation by other governmental sectors. Civil society, faith-based organizations, and the private sector are generally not included. Country-level partnerships should, therefore, include these nontraditional members, and the activities of these partner groups should be conducted under government ownership and leadership.

While some countries have set goals and targets in line with the health-related Millennium Development Goals, they are unlikely to achieve them on their own unless there is massive and sustained increase in development assistance from developed countries in order to help build national capacity for the successful large-scale implementation of programs in affected countries.

13. Secure affordable access to the latest medical and therapeutic discoveries

Development of sound policies to address the threat to health security due to the sharp increase in the prices of medicines and other commodities is required. To protect the poor nations from such a threat, such policies should envision a national patent regime to secure affordable access to the latest medical and therapeutic discoveries. Commitment is also required from the international community to alleviate the restrictive features of TRIPS in its application to the health sector.

14. Invest in research and development on malaria control tools

Safe and affordable antimalarial medicines for case management, as well as other medicines suitable for long-term prophylactic use or for intermittent preventive treatment of pregnant women and their young children, are lacking. Because *P. falciparum* is increasingly losing its susceptibility to chloroquine and SP, such effective therapies as those based on artemisinin (that is, ACTs) or other novel effective antimalarials recommended by WHO should be made available for treating uncomplicated malaria. Strong financial support will be required for developing and testing new antimalarial medicines. Large-scale cultivation in Africa of the plant that is the source of artemisinin, *Artemisia annua* (annual wormwood) and a process for safely extracting and formulating the active ingredient should be supported and subsidized.

Development of new or improved diagnostic methods that are simple, reliable, and readily applicable in the field should be supported.

The availability of antimalarial vaccines is long overdue; vaccines suitable for use by long-term residents of endemic sites and others for use by transient residents are required.

Antivector methods effective against adult as well as larval mosquitoes should be improved, and new classes of insecticides developed.

Basic and operational research should be conducted for malaria epidemic forecasting, prevention, early detection, and rapid response.

Estimated costs of scaled-up malaria control efforts in Ethiopia, 2005–15

Table A1.1

Population at risk for malaria by weight group in Ethiopia, 2005–15

Millions

Source: Center for National Health Development in Ethiopia 2004.

Description	Share of total population (percent)	2005	2006	2007	2008
Total population	100	73.0	75.1	77.2	77.4
Population at risk for malaria	68	49.7	51.1	52.5	52.6
Weight group (percentage of population at risk)					
5–<10 kg (1.9 percent)	2	0.9	1.0	1.0	1.0
10–<15 kg (6.8 percent)	7	3.4	3.5	3.6	3.6
15–<25 kg (16 percent)	16	7.9	8.2	8.4	8.4
25–<34 kg (8.3 percent)	8	4.1	4.2	4.4	4.4
≥34 kg (67 percent)	67	33.3	34.2	35.2	35.3

2009	2010	2011	2012	2013	2014	2015
81.4	83.5	85.9	89.3	91.8	94.5	97.2
55.4	56.8	58.4	60.7	62.5	64.3	66.1
1.1	1.1	1.1	1.2	1.2	1.2	1.3
3.8	3.9	4.0	4.1	4.2	4.4	4.5
8.9	9.1	9.3	9.7	10.0	10.3	10.6
4.6	4.7	4.8	5.0	5.2	5.3	5.5
37.1	38.0	39.1	40.7	41.8	43.1	44.3

Table A1.2
Total number of fever episodes by weight group in Ethiopia, 2005–15

Millions

Source: Center for National Health Development in Ethiopia 2004.

Description	2005	2006	2007	2008	2009	2010	2011	2012	2013	2014	2015
Estimated fever episodes											
5–<10 kg (1.9 percent) x 2 episodes	1.89	1.75	1.60	1.40	1.26	1.08	1.00	0.92	0.83	0.73	0.63
10–<15 kg (6.8 percent) x 2 episodes	6.75	6.25	5.71	5.01	4.52	3.86	3.57	3.30	2.97	2.62	2.25
15–<25 kg (16 percent) x 1.5 episodes	11.92	11.04	10.08	8.84	7.97	6.81	6.31	5.83	5.25	4.63	3.97
25–<34 kg (8.3 percent) x 1 episode	4.12	3.82	3.49	3.06	2.76	2.36	2.18	2.01	1.81	1.60	1.37
≥34 kg (67 percent) x 0.3 episode	9.98	9.24	8.44	7.40	6.68	5.71	5.28	4.88	4.39	3.87	3.32
Total	34.67	32.09	29.32	25.71	23.18	19.81	18.35	16.94	15.26	13.46	11.54
Estimated malaria cases by weight group (40 percent of total fever episodes assumed attributable to malaria)											
5–<10 kg (1.9 percent)	0.75	0.70	0.64	0.56	0.50	0.43	0.40	0.37	0.33	0.29	0.25
10–<15 kg (6.8 percent)	2.70	2.50	2.29	2.00	1.81	1.54	1.43	1.32	1.19	1.05	0.90
15–<25 kg (16 percent)	4.77	4.41	4.03	3.54	3.19	2.72	2.52	2.33	2.10	1.85	1.59
25–<34 kg (8.3 percent)	1.65	1.53	1.39	1.22	1.10	0.94	0.87	0.81	0.73	0.64	0.55
≥34 kg (67 percent)	3.99	3.70	3.38	2.96	2.67	2.28	2.11	1.95	1.76	1.55	1.33
Total	13.87	12.84	11.73	10.29	9.27	7.92	7.34	6.78	6.10	5.38	4.62
Estimated P. falciparum cases by weight group (70 percent of total malaria cases)											
5–<10 kg (1.9 percent)	0.53	0.49	0.45	0.39	0.35	0.30	0.28	0.26	0.23	0.21	0.18
10–<15 kg (6.8 percent)	1.89	1.75	1.60	1.40	1.26	1.08	1.00	0.92	0.83	0.73	0.63
15–<25 kg (16 percent)	3.34	3.09	2.82	2.48	2.23	1.91	1.77	1.63	1.47	1.30	1.11
25–<34 kg (8.3 percent)	1.15	1.07	0.98	0.86	0.77	0.66	0.61	0.56	0.51	0.45	0.38
≥34 kg (67 percent)	2.80	2.59	2.36	2.07	1.87	1.60	1.48	1.37	1.23	1.08	0.93
Total	9.71	8.99	8.21	7.20	6.49	5.55	5.14	4.74	4.27	3.77	3.23
Estimated P. vivax cases by weight group (30 percent of total malaria cases)											
5–<10 kg (1.9 percent)	0.23	0.21	0.19	0.17	0.15	0.13	0.12	0.11	0.10	0.09	0.08
10–<15 kg (6.8 percent)	0.81	0.75	0.69	0.60	0.54	0.46	0.43	0.40	0.36	0.31	0.27
15–<25 kg (16 percent)	1.43	1.32	1.21	1.06	0.96	0.82	0.76	0.70	0.63	0.56	0.48
25–<34 kg (8.3 percent)	0.49	0.46	0.42	0.37	0.33	0.28	0.26	0.24	0.22	0.19	0.16
≥34 kg (67 percent)	1.20	1.11	1.01	0.89	0.80	0.68	0.63	0.59	0.53	0.46	0.40
Total	4.16	3.85	3.52	3.09	2.78	2.38	2.20	2.03	1.83	1.61	1.38

Table A1.3
Management of uncomplicated malaria by treatment and weight group in Ethiopia, 2005–15

Source: Center for National Health Development in Ethiopia 2004.

Description	Quantity required	Cost per case (US$)	2005	2006	2007	2008	2009	2010	2011	2012	2013	2014	2015	Total costs
Number of weighted treatment doses of artemether-lumefantrine (ACT) required to treat uncomplicated P. falciparum malaria (millions)														
5–<10 kg (1.9 percent)	6 tabs/case	NA	3.17	2.94	2.68	2.35	2.12	1.81	1.68	1.55	1.40	1.23	1.06	
10–<15 kg (6.8 percent)	6 tabs/case	NA	11.35	10.51	9.60	8.42	7.59	6.48	6.01	5.55	4.99	4.40	3.78	
15–<25 kg (16 percent)	12 tabs/case	NA	40.05	37.08	33.87	29.71	26.78	22.89	21.20	19.58	17.63	15.55	13.33	
25–<34 kg (8.3 percent)	18 tabs/case	NA	20.78	19.23	17.57	15.41	13.89	11.87	11.00	10.16	9.14	8.06	6.92	
≥34 kg (67 percent)	24 tabs/case	NA	67.09	62.11	56.74	49.76	44.86	38.34	35.50	32.79	29.52	26.04	22.33	
Total ACT doses			142.43	131.86	120.47	105.64	95.24	81.40	75.38	69.62	62.68	55.29	47.41	
Number of weighted treatment doses of chloroquine required to treat P. vivax malaria (millions)														
5–<10 kg (1.9 percent)	4 tabs/case	NA	0.91	0.84	0.77	0.67	0.61	0.52	0.48	0.44	0.40	0.35	0.30	
10–<15 kg (6.8 percent)	4 tabs/case	NA	3.24	3.00	2.74	2.40	2.17	1.85	1.72	1.58	1.43	1.26	1.08	
15–<25 kg (16 percent)	8 tabs/case	NA	11.44	10.59	9.68	8.49	7.65	6.54	6.06	5.59	5.04	4.44	3.81	
25–<34 kg (8.3 percent)	10 tabs/case	NA	4.95	4.58	4.18	3.67	3.31	2.83	2.62	2.42	2.18	1.92	1.65	
≥34 kg (67 percent)	10 tabs/case	NA	11.98	11.09	10.13	8.89	8.01	6.85	6.34	5.86	5.27	4.65	3.99	
Total chloroquine doses			32.52	30.10	27.50	24.12	21.74	18.58	17.21	15.89	14.31	12.62	10.82	
Cost of artemether-lumefantrine tabs to treat uncomplicated P. falciparum malaria (US$ thousands)														
5–<10 kg (1.9 percent)	6 tabs/case	0.9	475.61	440.30	402.27	352.76	318.03	271.80	251.71	232.47	209.31	184.61	158.30	3,297.17
10–<15 kg (6.8 percent)	6 tabs/case	0.9	1,702.19	1,575.81	1,439.69	1,262.50	1,138.21	972.75	900.86	832.00	749.11	660.71	566.56	11,800.40
15–<25 kg (16 percent)	12 tabs/case	1.4	4,672.69	4,325.76	3,952.08	3,465.69	3,124.51	2,670.29	2,472.96	2,283.91	2,056.38	1,813.73	1,555.27	32,393.26
25–<34 kg (8.3 percent)	18 tabs/case	1.9	2,193.10	2,030.27	1,854.89	1,626.60	1,466.47	1,253.29	1,160.67	1,071.94	965.15	851.26	729.96	15,203.62
≥34 kg (67 percent)	24 tabs/case	2.4	6,708.65	6,210.55	5,674.06	4,975.73	4,485.90	3,833.78	3,550.46	3,279.05	2,952.37	2,603.99	2,232.92	46,507.47
Subtotal cost for treatment of *falciparum* malaria			15,752.25	14,582.69	13,322.99	11,683.28	10,533.13	9,001.90	8,336.66	7,699.37	6,932.32	6,114.31	5,243.02	109,201.92
Cost of chloroquine tablets to treat P. vivax malaria (US$ thousands)														
5–<10 kg (1.9 percent)	4 tabs/case	0.036	8.15	7.55	6.90	6.05	5.45	4.66	4.32	3.99	3.59	3.16	2.71	56.52
10–<15 kg (6.8 percent)	4 tabs/case	0.036	29.18	27.01	24.68	21.64	19.51	16.68	15.44	14.26	12.84	11.33	9.71	202.29
15–<25 kg (16 percent)	8 tabs/case	0.072	102.99	95.34	87.11	76.39	68.87	58.86	54.51	50.34	45.32	39.98	34.28	713.97

(continued on next page)

Table A1.3

Management of uncomplicated malaria by treatment and weight group in Ethiopia, 2005–15 *(continued)*

Description	Quantity required	Cost per case (US$)	2005	2006	2007	2008	2009	2010	2011	2012	2013	2014	2015	Total costs
25–<34 kg (8.3 percent)	10 tabs/case	0.09	44.52	41.22	37.66	33.02	29.77	25.44	23.56	21.76	19.59	17.28	14.82	308.64
≥34 kg (67 percent)	10 tabs/case	0.09	107.82	99.81	91.19	79.97	72.09	61.61	57.06	52.70	47.45	41.85	35.89	747.44
Subtotal cost of chloroquine tablets			292.66	270.93	247.53	217.07	195.70	167.25	154.89	143.05	128.80	113.60	97.41	2,028.88
Subtotal cost of chloroquine syrup to treat P. vivax malaria (US$ thousands)														
All cases under age 5	32.5 ml/case	0.05	35.36	32.74	29.91	26.23	23.65	20.21	18.71	17.28	15.56	13.73	11.77	245.14
Subtotal cost of premaquine for radical treatment of P. vivax malaria (US$ thousands)														
All cases age 5 and over	14 tablets/case	0.182	628.43	581.77	531.51	466.10	420.21	359.13	332.59	307.16	276.56	243.93	209.17	4,356.56
Subtotal cost for treatment of P. vivax malaria (US$ thousands)			956.45	885.44	808.95	709.39	639.56	546.58	506.19	467.49	420.92	371.25	318.35	6,630.57
Total cost for treatment of uncomplicated malaria (US$ thousands)			**16,708.70**	**15,468.13**	**14,131.94**	**12,392.67**	**11,172.69**	**9,548.48**	**8,842.85**	**8,166.86**	**7,353.24**	**6,485.56**	**5,561.37**	**115,832.49**

Table A1.4
Cost of managing severe malaria in Ethiopia, 2005–15
Dollars

Source: Center for National Health Development in Ethiopia 2004.

Description	Quantity required	Cost per case (US$)	2005	2006	2007	2008	2009	2010
Cost of quinine, 300 mg base (at 6 ampules per day for 3 days)	18 ampules/case	2.34	681,428.4	630,834.4	576,340.7	505,408.3	455,653.9	389,414.3
Cost of quinine, 300 mg base tablet (at 3 tablets per day for 7 days)	21 tablets/case	0.63	183,461.5	169,840.0	155,168.6	136,071.5	122,676.1	104,842.3
Cost of hospitilaztion for severe malaria	Per case	30	8,736,261.8	8,087,620.7	7,388,982.9	6,479,593.5	5,841,717.2	4,992,491.3
Total costs			9,601,151.7	8,888,295.1	8,120,492.2	7,121,073.3	6,420,047.2	5,486,748.0

Description	Quantity required	Cost per case (US$)	2011	2012	2013	2014	2015	Total costs
Cost of quinine, 300 mg base (at 6 ampules per day for 3 days)	18 ampules/case	2.34	360,636.6	333,067.9	299,886.0	264,499.5	226,808.3	4,723,978.5
Cost of quinine, 300 mg base tablet (at 3 tablets per day for 7 days)	21 tablets/case	0.63	97,094.5	89,672.1	80,738.6	71,211.4	61,063.8	1,271,840.4
Cost of hospitilaztion for severe malaria	Per case	30	4,623,546.2	4,270,101.8	3,844,692.9	3,391,019.2	2,907,798.9	60,563,826.5
Total costs			5,081,277.3	4,692,841.9	4,225,317.5	3,726,730.1	3,195,671.0	66,559,645.4

Table A1.5
Cost of intermittent preventive treatment of malaria during pregnancy, laboratory equipment and reagents (diagnosis), and antimalarial drug policy change and follow-up in Ethiopia, 2005–15

Dollars

Source: Center for National Health Development in Ethiopia 2004.

Description	Quantity required	Cost per unit (US$)	2005	2006	2007	2008	2009	2010	2011	2012	2013	2014	2015	Total costs
Intermittent preventive treatment of malaria during pregnancy														
Estimated female population in high-risk transmission areas			2,500,000	2,575,000	2,652,250	2,731,818	2,813,772	2,898,185	2,985,131	3,074,685	3,166,925	3,261,933	3,359,791	
Number of childbearing women (44 percent of women have a childbearing age of 15–44 years)			1,100,000	1,133,000	1,166,990	1,202,000	1,238,060	1,275,201	1,313,458	1,352,861	1,393,447	1,435,251	1,478,308	
Number of expected pregnancies per year (5 percent of childbearing women)			55,000	56,650	58,350	60,100	61,903	63,760	65,673	67,643	69,672	71,763	73,915	
Cost of sulfadoxine-pyrimethamine required for use at health facilities and communities ($0.08 per dose)	2 doses/woman	0.16	8,800	9,064	9,336	9,616	9,904	10,202	10,508	10,823	11,148	11,482	11,826	112,709
Costs of laboratory equipment and reagents (30 percent of total fever episodes diagnosed with microscopy) (US$)														
Providing microscopes to hospitals in each region	119	2,130	253,470											253,470
Providing each district health center with microscopes (3 per district in 453 districts)	1,359	2,130	2,894,670											2,894,670
Reagents (such as giemsa), microslides, and other supplies			4,160,125	3,851,248	3,518,563	3,085,521	2,781,770	2,377,377	2,201,689	2,033,382	1,830,806	1,614,771	1,384,666	28,839,917
Costs of rapid diagnostic tests at peripheral and community levels (US$)														
Rapid diagnostic tests at peripheral health facility and community levels with no microscopy (70 percent of total fever episodes)		0.61	14,803,110	13,704,024	12,520,221	10,979,311	9,898,465	8,459,499	7,834,342	7,235,450	6,514,619	5,745,894	4,927,104	102,622,039
Subtotal			22,111,375	17,555,272	16,038,784	14,064,832	12,680,235	10,836,876	10,036,031	9,268,832	8,345,425	7,360,665	6,311,770	134,610,097
Costs of antimalarial drug policy change and follow-up (US$)														
Consult with stakeholders on the status of resistance to antimalarial drugs (based on data)			50,000			50,000			50,000			50,000		200,000
Formulate policy for changing to new artemisinin-based combination therapy (ACT) antimalarial drugs			50,000											

Description	Quantity required	Cost per unit (US$)	2005	2006	2007	2008	2009	2010	2011	2012	2013	2014	2015	Total costs
Adopt and approve the policy for implementation			15,000											
Develop treatment guidelines based on the approved policy for use by public and private health services, NGOs, and others			50,000											
Distribute and supply ACT			150,000			150,000			150,000			150,000		600,000
Public campaign to create awareness among the public; media, posters, pamphlets on ACT use and compliance			100,000	100,000	100,000	100,000	100,000	100,000	100,000	100,000	100,000	100,000	100,000	1,100,000
Monitor for effectiveness of ACT under field conditions and for possible side effects			150,000	150,000	150,000	150,000	150,000	150,000	150,000	150,000	150,000	150,000	150,000	1,650,000
Subtotal			565,000	250,000	250,000	450,000	250,000	250,000	450,000	250,000	250,000	450,000	250,000	3,550,000
Total costs			22,685,175	17,814,336	16,298,120	14,524,448	12,940,140	11,097,078	10,496,539	9,529,655	8,606,572	7,822,147	6,573,596	138,387,805

Table A1.6
Selective vector control in Ethiopia, 2005–15

Source: Center for National Health Development in Ethiopia 2004.

Description	Cost per unit (US$)	2005	2006	2007	2008	2009	2010	2011	2012	2013	2014	2015	Total costs
Long-lasting insecticide-treated bednets (millions)													
Total population at risk		49.7	51.1	52.5	52.6	55.4	56.8	58.4	60.7	62.5	64.3	66.1	
Total population eligible for insecticide-treated bednets		14.9	8.6	3.9	6.7	6.0	4.3	7.2	6.1	4.8	7.8	6.6	
Number of households (population at risk/5 people)		3.0	1.7	0.8	1.3	1.2	0.9	1.4	1.2	1.0	1.6	1.3	
Number of long-lasting insecticide-treated bednets (3 per household) to reach total population at risk		8.9	5.2	2.3	4.0	3.6	2.6	4.3	3.6	2.9	4.7	4.0	
Expected coverage per year (percent)		45	60	90	100	100	100	100	100	100	100	100	
Total insecticide-treated bednets required per year based on coverage		4.0	3.1	2.1	4.0	3.6	2.6	4.3	3.6	2.9	4.7	4.0	
Indoor residual spraying of houses (millions)													
Population to be protect through indoor residual spraying (60 percent of the total population live in unstable transmission area)		29.8	30.7	31.5	31.6	33.2	34.1	35.0	36.4	37.5	38.6	39.7	
Number of households targeted for indoor residual spraying (population/5 people)		6.0	6.1	6.3	6.3	6.6	6.8	7.0	7.3	7.5	7.7	7.9	
Number of unit structures to be sprayed (3 unit structures per household)		17.9	18.4	18.9	18.9	19.9	20.4	21.0	21.8	22.5	23.1	23.8	
Average surface area of unit structure to be sprayed, at 100 square meters/unit structure (square meters)		1,788.0	1,839.2	1,890.3	1,894.5	1,992.7	2,043.6	2,102.9	2,184.9	2,248.2	2,313.4	2,380.5	
Insecticide required at a dose of 2.67 gm (0.00267 kg) per square meter (grams)		4.8	4.9	5.0	5.1	5.3	5.5	5.6	5.8	6.0	6.2	6.4	
Insecticide actual plus 10 percent safety margin (kilograms)		5.3	5.4	5.6	5.6	5.9	6.0	6.2	6.4	6.6	6.8	7.0	
Human resource requirement for indoor residual spraying (thousands)													
Number of spray persons (total houses divided by 360 person-days)		16.56	17.03	17.50	17.54	18.45	18.92	19.47	20.23	20.82	21.42	22.04	
Number of squads (1 squad per 5 spray persons)		3.31	3.41	3.50	3.51	3.69	3.78	3.89	4.05	4.16	4.28	4.41	
Number of teams or technicians (1 team per 5 squads)		0.66	0.68	0.70	0.70	0.74	0.76	0.78	0.81	0.83	0.86	0.88	
Number of supervisors (1 supervisor per 5 teams)		0.13	0.14	0.14	0.14	0.15	0.15	0.16	0.16	0.17	0.17	0.18	

Description	Cost per unit (US$)	2005	2006	2007	2008	2009	2010	2011	2012	2013	2014	2015	Total costs
Cost of insecticide-treated bednets (US$ millions)													
Total cost of long-lasting insecticide-treated bednets	5	20.12	15.52	10.45	20.22	17.95	12.90	21.70	18.23	14.48	23.33	19.90	194.79
Handling, storage, and distribution cost	2	8.05	6.21	4.18	8.09	7.18	5.16	8.68	7.29	5.79	9.33	7.96	77.92
Cost of retreatment for existing retreatable insecticide-treated bednets (3 million bednets)	0.4	1.20											1.20
Subtotal for insecticide-treated bednets		29.36	21.73	14.63	28.31	25.13	18.06	30.38	25.52	20.27	32.66	27.86	273.91
Cost of insecticide and spray pumps (US$ millions)													
Cost of insecticide	4.3	22.58	23.23	23.87	23.93	25.17	25.81	26.56	27.59	28.39	29.22	30.06	286.41
Spray pumps and spare parts	500	24.83	0.00	0.00	0.00	0.00	6.21	0.00	0.00	0.00	0.00	0.00	31.04
Subtotal cost of insecticide and spray pumps		47.41	23.23	23.87	23.93	25.17	32.02	26.56	27.59	28.39	29.22	30.06	317.45
Cost of human power (US$ millions)													
Wage for spray persons (40 days plus 6 training days)	10	7.62	7.83	8.05	8.07	8.49	8.70	8.96	9.31	9.58	9.85	10.14	96.59
Wage for squad chiefs (40 person-days plus 6 training days)	15	2.28	2.35	2.42	2.42	2.55	2.61	2.69	2.79	2.87	2.96	3.04	28.98
Wage for technicians (40 person-days plus 6 training days)	15	0.46	0.47	0.48	0.48	0.51	0.52	0.54	0.56	0.57	0.59	0.61	5.80
Wage for supervisors (18 person-days)	20	0.05	0.05	0.05	0.05	0.05	0.05	0.06	0.06	0.06	0.06	0.06	0.60
Per diem for regional supervisors or coordinators (2 persons per region)	25	0.01	0.01	0.01	0.01	0.01	0.01	0.01	0.01	0.01	0.01	0.01	0.10
Forms and stationery (per house)	0.06	0.36	0.37	0.38	0.38	0.40	0.41	0.42	0.44	0.45	0.46	0.48	4.54
Subtotal cost of human power		10.77	11.08	11.39	11.41	12.00	12.31	12.67	13.16	13.54	13.93	14.34	136.60
Field equipment (US$ millions)													
Tents (4-person fly tents per team and supervisors)	2,000	1.59	1.63	1.68	1.68	1.77	1.82	1.87	1.94	2.00	2.06	2.12	20.16
Coveralls, hand gloves, goggles, buckets, soaps, and the like for spray persons, squad chiefs, technicians, and other personnel	100	2.05	2.11	2.17	2.18	2.29	2.35	2.41	2.51	2.58	2.66	2.73	26.04

(continued on next page)

Table A1.6

Selective vector control in Ethiopia, 2005–15

(continued)

Description	Cost per unit (US$)	2005	2006	2007	2008	2009	2010	2011	2012	2013	2014	2015	Total costs
Spray operation logistics (3 pickups and 2 trucks per district to transport equipment and personnel)	125,000	37.50	25.29	25.29	25.29	25.29	6.39	6.39	6.39	6.39	6.39	6.39	177.02
Spare parts and maintenance (15 percent of total cost)	18,750	5.63	3.79	3.79	3.79	3.79	3.79	3.79	3.79	3.79	3.79	3.79	43.56
Fuel and lubricant (per day per team and supervisor plus travel days for 300 districts)	3,000	0.90	0.90	0.90	0.90	0.90	0.90	0.90	0.90	0.90	0.90	0.90	9.90
Insurance for the spraying team and vehicles		2.00	2.00	2.00	2.00	2.00	2.00	2.00	2.00	2.00	2.00	2.00	22.00
Subtotal		49.67	35.73	35.83	35.84	36.04	17.25	17.37	17.54	17.67	17.80	17.94	298.67
Larviciding using Temephos and environmental management in urban and development areas (US$ millions)													
Abate (20 barrels per region for 9 regions)	120	0.02	0.02	0.02	0.02	0.02	0.02	0.02	0.02	0.02	0.02	0.02	0.24
Environmental management through community participation	500	0.23	0.23	0.23	0.23	0.23	0.23	0.23	0.23	0.23	0.23	0.23	2.45
Subtotal		0.25	0.25	0.25	0.25	0.25	0.25	0.25	0.25	0.25	0.25	0.25	2.73
Total cost for vector control		137.46	92.01	85.97	99.74	98.59	79.88	87.22	84.05	80.12	93.86	90.45	

Table A1.7

Epidemic prevention and control; information, education, and communication; advocacy; behavioral change; and monitoring and evaluation in Ethiopia, 2005–15

Source: Center for National Health Development in Ethiopia 2004.

Dollars

Description	Quantity required	Cost per unit (US$)	2005	2006	2007	2008	2009	2010	2011	2012	2013	2014	2015	Total costs
Epidemic prevention and control														
Mapping and stratifying malarious areas of the country			200,000	200,000										400,000
Procuring ground weather stations for 300 epidemic-prone districts	300	1,000	300,000	50,000	50,000	50,000	50,000	50,000	50,000	50,000	50,000	50,000	50,000	800,000
Strengthening surveillance information system of each *wereda* (district and region) for monitoring	453	300	135,900	135,900	135,900	135,900	135,900	135,900	135,900	135,900	135,900	135,900	135,900	1,494,900
Epidemic preparedness and response: cost of drugs, insecticides, and operational cost for epidemic response			3,000,000	3,000,000	3,000,000	3,000,000	3,000,000	3,000,000	3,000,000	3,000,000	3,000,000	3,000,000	3,000,000	33,000,000
Total cost for epidemic prevention and control			3,635,900	3,385,900	3,185,900	3,185,900	3,185,900	3,185,900	3,185,900	3,185,900	3,185,900	3,185,900	3,185,900	35,694,900
Information, education, and communication; advocacy; and behavioral change														
Producing information, education, and communication materials targeting health workers, community leaders, and communities			100,000	100,000	100,000	100,000	100,000	100,000	100,000	100,000	100,000	100,000	100,000	1,100,000
Radio spots, television, drama and other educational media to increase treatment-seeking behavior, compliance, and use of insecticide-treated nets			50,000	50,000	50,000	50,000	50,000	50,000	50,000	50,000	50,000	50,000	50,000	550,000
Sensitization and advocacy meeting at district, regional, and national levels	464	1,000	464,000	464,000	464,000	464,000	464,000	464,000	464,000	464,000	464,000	464,000	464,000	5,104,000
Total cost for information, education, and communication; advocacy; and behavioral change			614,000	614,000	614,000	614,000	614,000	614,000	614,000	614,000	614,000	614,000	614,000	6,754,000
Monitoring and evaluation														
Quarterly district review meetings to monitor progress of community and peripheral level health facilities program activities	453	1,000	453,000	453,000	453,000	453,000	453,000	453,000	453,000	453,000	453,000	453,000	453,000	4,983,000
Annual regional review meeting (3 participants per district)	11	2,571	28,280	28,280	28,280	28,280	28,280	28,280	28,280	28,280	28,280	28,280	28,280	311,080
Routine supervision (regional and district levels)	460	2,000	920,000	920,000	920,000	920,000	920,000	920,000	920,000	920,000	920,000	920,000	920,000	10,120,000
Annual national meeting to review progress and develop implementation plan of action (regional health bureaus, federal ministry of health, RBM partners, academic institutions, NGOs, private sector, and civil societies) (50 participants)		3,000	3,000	3,000	3,000	3,000	3,000	3,000	3,000	3,000	3,000	3,000	3,000	33,000
Total cost for monitoring and evaluation			1,404,280	1,404,280	1,404,280	1,404,280	1,404,280	1,404,280	1,404,280	1,404,280	1,404,280	1,404,280	1,404,280	15,447,080

Table A1.8
Institutional strengthening and human resource capacity building in Ethiopia, 2005–15

Dollars

Source: Center for National Health Development in Ethiopia 2004.

Description	Quantity required	Cost per unit (US$)	2005	2006	2007	2008	2009	2010	2011	2012	2013	2014	2015	Total costs
Institutional strengthening														
Strengthening national training center	1	100,000	100,000	25,000	25,000	25,000	25,000	25,000	25,000	25,000	25,000	25,000	25,000	350,000
Establishing regional training centers	10	50,000	500,000	10,000	10,000	10,000	10,000	10,000	10,000	10,000	10,000	10,000	10,000	600,000
Establishing entomology laboratory and insectory	1	50,000	50,000	15,000	15,000	15,000	15,000	15,000	15,000	15,000	15,000	15,000	15,000	200,000
Establishing national malaria diagnostics and quality control center	1	100,000	100,000	30,000	30,000	30,000	30,000	30,000	30,000	30,000	30,000	30,000	30,000	400,000
Strengthening national and regional training schools by incorporating malaria prevention and control strategies into curricula			100,000	100,000				100,000	100,000					400,000
Strengthening vocational training centers for health extension programs	17	50,000	850,000	850,000	850,000	850,000	850,000	850,000	850,000	850,000	850,000	850,000	850,000	9,350,000
Subtotal			1,700,000	1,030,000	930,000	930,000	930,000	1,030,000	1,030,000	930,000	930,000	930,000	930,000	11,300,000
Health extension package														
Training of health extension workers (for 12 months at $200 per month)	36,000	2,400	21,600,000	12,600,000	12,600,000	12,600,000	12,600,000	2,400,000	2,400,000	2,400,000	2,400,000	2,400,000	2,400,000	86,400,000
Training of community health workers and community health promoters (for 8 days at $10 per day)	180,000	80	3,600,000	2,100,000	2,100,000	2,100,000	2,100,000	400,000	400,000	400,000	400,000	400,000	400,000	14,400,000
Subtotal			25,200,000	14,700,000	14,700,000	14,700,000	14,700,000	2,800,000	2,800,000	2,800,000	2,800,000	2,800,000	2,800,000	100,800,000
Refresher training of existing health workers (person-days)														
Training regional trainers on planning and malaria prevention (for 30 days at $20 per day, twice during 2005–15)	3,000	600	1,800,000					1,800,000						3,600,000
Training health workers on case management (5-day sessions, 8 health														

Description	required	unit (US$)	2005	2006	2007	2008	2009	2010	2011	2012	2013	2014	2015	Total costs
Training district health staff personnel on vector control including epidemic prevention and control (5-day sessions for 8 workers per district for 453 districts)	18,120	10	181,200	18,120	18,120	18,120	18,120	18,120	18,120	18,120	18,120	18,120	18,120	362,400
Training laboratory technicians on basic malaria microscopy (5-day sessions for 3 technicians per district)	6,795	10	67,950	6,795	6,795	6,795	6,795	6,795	6,795	6,795	6,795	6,795	6,795	135,900
Workshop on planning of malaria control including epidemic preparedness and malaria control in 453 malarious districts (3 persons per district for 5-day sessions)	6,795	10	67,950	6,795	6,795	6,795	6,795	6,795	6,795	6,795	6,795	6,795	6,795	135,900
Subtotal for in-service refresher training			558,300	49,830	49,830	49,830	49,830	109,830	49,830	49,830	49,830	49,830	49,830	1,116,600
Capacity building by recruiting additional staff														
Recruiting epidemiologists at the regional level (2 per region)	20	6,000	120,000	120,000	120,000	120,000	120,000	120,000	120,000	120,000	120,000	120,000	120,000	1,320,000
Recruiting 1 entomologist, 1 epidemiologist, 1 medical officer, and 1 statistician at the federal level	3	6,000	18,000	18,000	18,000	18,000	18,000	18,000	18,000	18,000	18,000	18,000	18,000	198,000
Strengthen district offices by recruiting 3 staff members for each district (1 in vector control, 1 in case management, and 1 in social mobilization or information, education, and communication)	1,359	2,820	3,832,380	3,832,380	3,832,380	3,832,380	3,832,380	3,832,380	3,832,380	3,832,380	3,832,380	3,832,380	3,832,380	42,156,180
Subtotal for additional staff			3,970,380	3,970,380	3,970,380	3,970,380	3,970,380	3,970,380	3,970,380	3,970,380	3,970,380	3,970,380	3,970,380	43,674,180
Retaining existing malaria staff by paying a top-up salary														
Top-up salary for medical officers (base salary $2,091 per year)	1,280	7,909	10,123,520	10,123,520	10,123,520	10,123,520	10,123,520	10,123,520	10,123,520	10,123,520	10,123,520	10,123,520	10,123,520	111,358,720
Top-up salary for epidemiologists (base salary $2,091 per year)	82	7,909	648,538	648,538	648,538	648,538	648,538	648,538	648,538	648,538	648,538	648,538	648,538	7,133,918
Top-up salary for entomologists (base salary $2,091 per year)	20	7,909	158,180	158,180	158,180	158,180	158,180	158,180	158,180	158,180	158,180	158,180	158,180	1,739,980
Top-up salary for biologists (base salary $2,091 per year)	28	4,909	137,452	137,452	137,452	137,452	137,452	137,452	137,452	137,452	137,452	137,452	137,452	1,511,972

(continued on next page)

Table A1.8

Institutional strengthening and human resource capacity building in Ethiopia, 2005–15

Dollars

(continued)

Description	Quantity required	Cost per unit (US$)	2005	2006	2007	2008	2009	2010	2011	2012	2013	2014	2015	Total costs
Top-up salary for health officers (base salary $2,091 per year)	631	4,909	3,097,579	3,097,579	3,097,579	3,097,579	3,097,579	3,097,579	3,097,579	3,097,579	3,097,579	3,097,579	3,097,579	34,073,369
Top-up salary for nurses (base salary $836 per year)	14,160	3,164	44,802,240	44,802,240	44,802,240	44,802,240	44,802,240	44,802,240	44,802,240	44,802,240	44,802,240	44,802,240	44,802,240	492,824,640
Top-up salary for environment health workers (base salary $836 per year)	1,054	2,164	2,280,856	2,280,856	2,280,856	2,280,856	2,280,856	2,280,856	2,280,856	2,280,856	2,280,856	2,280,856	2,280,856	25,089,416
Top-up salary for malaria technicians (laboratory, entomology, operations) (base salary $697 per year)	2,145	1,303	2,794,935	2,794,935	2,794,935	2,794,935	2,794,935	2,794,935	2,794,935	2,794,935	2,794,935	2,794,935	2,794,935	30,744,285
Subtotal for in-service top-up salary			64,043,300	64,043,300	64,043,300	64,043,300	64,043,300	64,043,300	64,043,300	64,043,300	64,043,300	64,043,300	64,043,300	704,476,300
Total cost for institutional strengthening and human resource capacity building			95,471,980	83,793,510	83,693,510	83,693,510	83,693,510	71,953,510	71,893,510	71,793,510	71,793,510	71,793,510	71,793,510	861,367,080

Table A1.9
Operational research activities in Ethiopia, 2005–15
Dollars

Source: Center for National Health Development in Ethiopia 2004.

Description	Quantity required	Cost per unit (US$)	2005	2006	2007	2008	2009	2010	2011	2012	2013	2014	2015	Total costs
Funding for epidemiological, entomological, and social-behavioral surveys	4	100,000	400,000				400,000				400,000		400,000	1,600,000
Developing guidelines for treatment, indoor residual spraying, insecticide-treated bednets, epidemics, environmental management, and community-based interventions	6	20,000	120,000					120,000						240,000
Monitoring antimalarial drug efficacy studies in 14 sentinel sites	14	5,000	70,000				70,000				70,000			210,000
Monitoring insecticide resistance in 4 sites	4	10,000	40,000				40,000				40,000			120,000
Knowledge, attitude, and practices survey on health extension programs in 5 sites	5	20,000	100,000			100,000			100,000				100,000	400,000
Evaluating outcome of planned activities in 10 regions	10	20,000	200,000					200,000					200,000	600,000
Impact assessment in 10 regions	10	20,000						200,000					200,000	400,000
Total cost for operational research activities			930,000			100,000	510,000	520,000	100,000		510,000		900,000	3,570,000

Table A1.10

Program management costs in Ethiopia, 2005–15

Dollars

Source: Center for National Health Development in Ethiopia 2004.

Description	Quantity required	Cost per unit (US$)	2005	2006	2007	2008	2009	2010	2011	2012	2013	2014	2015	Total costs
District level														
Strengthening district health offices through data and health management information systems	453	5,000	2,265,000	453,000	453,000	453,000	453,000	453,000	453,000	453,000	453,000	453,000	453,000	6,795,000
Four-wheel drive pickup (1 per district)	453	25,000	11,325,000											11,325,000
Spare parts (15 percent of total cost per year)	453	3,750		1,698,750	1,698,750	1,698,750	1,698,750	1,698,750	1,698,750	1,698,750	1,698,750	1,698,750	1,698,750	16,987,500
Fuel and maintenance for pickups	453	1,000	453,000	453,000	453,000	453,000	453,000	453,000	453,000	453,000	453,000	453,000	453,000	4,983,000
Motorcycles (for rugged terrain) for 453 district health management offices	1,359	5,000	6,795,000					6,795,000						13,590,000
Spare parts (15 percent of total cost per year)	453	750		339,750	339,750	339,750	339,750	339,750	339,750	339,750	339,750	339,750	339,750	3,397,500
Fuel and maintenance for motorcycles (for district health management offices)	453	500	226,500	226,500	226,500	226,500	226,500	226,500	226,500	226,500	226,500	226,500	226,500	2,491,500
Motorcycles for extension health workers (1 per person)	30,000	5,000	45,000,000	26,250,000	26,250,000	26,250,000	26,250,000	500,000	500,000	500,000	500,000	500,000	500,000	153,000,000
Fuel and maintenance for motorcycles (for extension health workers)	30,000	300	9,000,000	9,000,000	9,000,000	9,000,000	9,000,000	9,000,000	9,000,000	9,000,000	9,000,000	9,000,000	9,000,000	99,000,000
Spare parts (15 percent of total cost per year)				3,937,500	3,937,500	3,937,500	3,937,500	3,937,500	3,937,500	3,937,500	3,937,500	3,937,500	3,937,500	
Registration book and stationery for 30,000 extension health workers and						1,800	1,800	1,800	1,800	1,800	1,800	1,800	1,800	15,760,800

Description	Quantity required	Cost per unit (US$)	2005	2006	2007	2008	2009	2010	2011	2012	2013	2014	2015	Total costs
Administrative costs			500,000	500,000	500,000	500,000	500,000	500,000	500,000	500,000	500,000	500,000	500,000	5,500,000
Subtotal for district level			75,624,500	42,918,500	42,918,500	42,918,500	42,918,500	20,067,800	13,272,800	13,272,800	13,272,800	13,272,800	13,272,800	333,730,300
Regional level														
Strengthening regional offices through data and health management information systems	10	10,000	100,000	20,000	20,000	20,000	20,000	20,000	20,000	20,000	20,000	20,000	20,000	300,000
Four-wheel-drive station wagon (2 per region)	20	50,000	1,000,000											1,000,000
Spare parts (15 percent of total cost per year)	20	7,500		150,000	150,000	150,000	150,000	150,000	150,000	150,000	150,000	150,000	150,000	1,500,000
Fuel and maintenance for four-wheel-drive station wagon	20	5,000	100,000	100,000	100,000	100,000	100,000	100,000	100,000	100,000	100,000	100,000	100,000	1,100,000
Administrative costs			250,000	250,000	250,000	250,000	250,000	250,000	250,000	250,000	250,000	250,000	250,000	2,750,000
Subtotal for regional level			1,450,000	520,000	520,000	520,000	520,000	520,000	520,000	520,000	520,000	520,000	520,000	6,650,000
National level														
Strengthening national program through data and health management information system	1	15,000	15,000	3,000	3,000	3,000	3,000	3,000	3,000	3,000	3,000	3,000	3,000	45,000
Four-wheel-drive station wagon (2 at national level)	2	50,000	100,000											100,000
Spare parts (15 percent of total cost per year)	2	7,500		15,000	15,000	15,000	15,000	15,000	15,000	15,000	15,000	15,000	15,000	150,000
Fuel and maintenance for four-wheel-drive station wagon	2	10,000	20,000	20,000	20,000	20,000	20,000	20,000	20,000	20,000	20,000	20,000	20,000	220,000
Administrative costs			25,000	25,000	25,000	25,000	25,000	25,000	25,000	25,000	25,000	25,000	25,000	275,000
Subtotal for national level			160,000	63,000	63,000	63,000	63,000	63,000	63,000	63,000	63,000	63,000	63,000	790,000
Total cost for program management			77,234,500	43,501,500	43,501,500	43,501,500	43,501,500	20,650,800	13,855,800	13,855,800	13,855,800	13,855,800	13,855,800	341,170,300

Table A1.11
Summary costs of malaria prevention and control in Ethiopia, 2005–15

Dollars

Source: Center for National Health Development in Ethiopia 2004.

Category	2005	2006	2007	2008	2009	2010	2011	2012	2013	2014	2015	Total costs
Management of uncomplicated malaria	16,708,703	15,468,132	14,131,939	12,392,669	11,172,687	9,548,484	8,842,851	8,166,864	7,353,240	6,485,558	5,561,366	115,832,493
Treatment of *P. falciparum* malaria	15,752,250	14,582,693	13,322,988	11,683,279	10,533,131	9,001,902	8,336,662	7,699,370	6,932,320	6,114,307	5,243,018	109,201,920
Treatment of *P. vivax* malaria	956,452	885,439	808,951	709,391	639,556	546,582	506,189	467,494	420,920	371,251	318,348	6,630,573
Management of severe malaria	9,601,152	8,888,295	8,120,492	7,121,073	6,420,047	5,486,748	5,081,277	4,692,842	4,225,318	3,726,730	3,195,671	66,559,645
Intermittent preventive treatment of malaria during pregnancy	8,800	9,064	9,336	9,616	9,904	10,202	10,508	10,823	11,148	11,482	11,826	112,709
Laboratory equipment and reagents (diagnosis)	22,111,375	17,555,272	16,038,784	14,064,832	12,680,235	10,836,876	10,036,031	9,268,832	8,345,425	7,360,665	6,311,770	134,610,097
Antimalarial drug policy change and follow-up	565,000	250,000	250,000	450,000	250,000	250,000	450,000	250,000	250,000	450,000	250,000	3,665,000
Vector control (prevention)	137,462,888	92,010,866	85,973,148	99,736,191	98,589,810	79,881,116	87,222,932	84,054,198	80,123,343	93,860,627	90,449,402	1,029,364,520
Insecticide-treated bednets	29,361,302	21,726,049	14,630,000	28,306,958	25,130,000	18,056,889	30,381,203	25,516,032	20,274,527	32,663,153	27,864,159	273,910,272
Insecticide and spray pumps	47,414,673	23,227,218	23,873,364	23,925,921	25,165,654	32,017,108	26,557,160	27,592,889	28,393,083	29,216,482	30,063,760	317,447,313
Human power (indoor residual spraying)	10,771,551	11,079,516	11,387,480	11,412,530	12,003,409	12,309,900	12,666,627	13,160,274	13,541,661	13,934,108	14,337,936	136,604,993
Field equipment	49,667,261	35,729,983	35,834,204	35,842,681	36,042,647	17,249,119	17,369,843	17,536,903	17,665,972	17,798,784	17,935,447	298,672,843
Larviciding and environmental management	248,100	248,100	248,100	248,100	248,100	248,100	248,100	248,100	248,100	248,100	248,100	2,729,100
Epidemic prevention and control	3,635,900	3,385,900	3,185,900	3,185,900	3,185,900	3,185,900	3,185,900	3,185,900	3,185,900	3,185,900	3,185,900	35,694,900
Advocacy; information, education, and communication; and behavioral change	614,000	614,000	614,000	614,000	614,000	614,000	614,000	614,000	614,000	614,000	614,000	6,754,000
Monitoring and evaluation	1,404,280	1,404,280	1,404,280	1,404,280	1,404,280	1,404,280	1,404,280	1,404,280	1,404,280	1,404,280	1,404,280	15,447,080
Institutional strengthening and human resource capacity building	95,471,980	83,793,510	83,693,510	83,693,510	83,693,510	71,953,510	71,893,510	71,793,510	71,793,510	71,793,510	71,793,510	861,367,080
Institutional strengthening	1,700,000	1,030,000	930,000	930,000	930,000	1,030,000	1,030,000	930,000	930,000	930,000	930,000	11,300,000
Health extension program	25,200,000	14,700,000	14,700,000	14,700,000	14,700,000	2,800,000	2,800,000	2,800,000	2,800,000	2,800,000	2,800,000	100,800,000
Refresher training for health workers	558,300	49,830	49,830	49,830	49,830	109,830	49,830	49,830	49,830	49,830	49,830	1,116,600
Capacity building by recruiting additional staff	3,970,380	3,970,380	3,970,380	3,970,380	3,970,380	3,970,380	3,970,380	3,970,380	3,970,380	3,970,380	3,970,380	43,674,180
Retaining malaria staff by topping up salary	64,043,300	64,043,300	64,043,300	64,043,300	64,043,300	64,043,300	64,043,300	64,043,300	64,043,300	64,043,300	64,043,300	704,476,300
Operational research activities	930,000			100,000	510,000	520,000	100,000		510,000		900,000	3,570,000
Program management	77,234,500	43,501,500	43,501,500	43,501,500	43,501,500	20,650,800	13,855,800	13,855,800	13,855,800	13,855,800	13,855,800	341,170,300
District level	75,624,500	42,918,500	42,918,500	42,918,500	42,918,500	20,067,800	13,272,800	13,272,800	13,272,800	13,272,800	13,272,800	333,730,300
Regional level	1,450,000	520,000	520,000	520,000	520,000	520,000	520,000	520,000	520,000	520,000	520,000	6,650,000
National level	160,000	63,000	63,000	63,000	63,000	63,000	63,000	63,000	63,000	63,000	63,000	790,000

Table A1.12

Underlying assumptions for calculating requirements for malaria prevention and control in Ethiopia (organized by table)

Source: Center for National Health Development in Ethiopia 2004.

Description	Assumption	Unit or value
Administrative divisions	11 regional states and 606 districts	
Malarious districts	453 out of 606 (74.5 percent)	
Underlying assumptions for table A1.1—Population		
Population	Taken from projection based on 1994 census, starting in 2004	71,133,749
Population at risk for malaria	68 percent of the total population starting in 2004	48,370,949
Objective of malaria control in Ethiopia	Reduce malaria burden by half by 2010 and by a further 50 percent by 2015	
Population growth	3 percent per year	
Population by age and weight category	Age	
5–<10 kg (1.9 percent)	0–<1 year	
10–<15 kg (6.8 percent)	1–<3 years	
15–<25 kg (16 percent)	3–<10 years	
25–<34 kg (8.3 percent)	10–<15 years	
≥34 kg (67 percent)	≥15 years	
Underlying assumptions for table A1.2—Number of fever episodes and malaria cases		
Number of fever episodes per year per person by age category		
5–<10 kg (1.9 percent)	2 episodes	
10–<15 kg (6.8 percent)	2 episodes	
15–<25 kg (16 percent)	1.5 episodes	
25–<34 kg (8.3 percent)	1 episodes	
≥34 kg (67 percent)	0.3 episodes	
Total number of fever episodes per year in the population at risk	30 percent of all population at risk	
Proportion of fever episodes attributable to malaria	40 percent of all febrile episodes	
Proportion of *P. falciparum* malaria	70 percent of all malaria cases	
Proportion of *P. vivax* malaria	30 percent of all malaria cases	
Yearly reduction of fever morbidity as malaria treatment and prevention improves	10 percent less of the population at risk during the preceding year plus the added population at risk in that year	
Underlying assumptions for table A1.3—Antimalarial drugs and case management		
Unit price for full treatment doses of artemther-lumefantrine per case of uncomplicated *P. falciparum* malaria by age and weight		
5–<10 kg (1.9 percent)	6 tablets/case	$0.90 per case
10–<15 kg (6.8 percent)	6 tablets/case	$0.90 per case
15–<25 kg (16 percent)	12 tablets/case	$1.40 per case
25–<34 kg (8.3 percent)	18 tablets/case	$1.90 per case
≥34 kg (67 percent)	24 tablets/case	$2.40 per case

(continued on next page)

Table A1.12

**Underlying
assumptions
for calculating
requirements for
malaria prevention
and control in Ethiopia
(organized by table)**

(continued)

Description	Assumption	Unit or value
Unit price for full treatment doses of chloroquine per case of uncomplicated *P. vivax* malaria by age and weight		
5–<10 kg (1.9 percent)	4 tablets/case	$0.036/case
10–<15 kg (6.8 percent)	4 tablets/case	$0.036/case
15–<25 kg (16 percent)	8 tablets/case	$0.072/case
25–<34 kg (8.3 percent)	10 tablets/case	$0.090/case
≥34 kg (67 percent)	10 tablets/case	$0.090/case
Unit cost of chloroquine syrup for treatment of *P. vivax* malaria cases under age five (17 percent of all *vivax* malaria cases)	32.5 ml/case	$0.05/case
Unit cost of premaquine for radical treatment of *P. vivax* malaria cases over age five (83 percent of all *vivax* malaria cases)	14 tablets/case (1 tablet/day for 14 days)	$0.182/case
Percentage of severe malaria cases	3 percent of *P. falciparum* cases	
Underlying assumptions for table A1.4—Treatment for severe malaria		
Unit cost per full treatment of severe malaria case using quinine 300 mg base (6 ampules per day for 3 days)	Box of 100 ampules ($13) 18 ampules/case	$2.34/case
Unit cost of follow-up treatment for severe malaria case using quinine 300 mg tablets (3 tablets per day for 7 days)	Tin of 1,000 tablets ($30) 21 ampules/case	$0.63/case
Cost of hospitalization for severe malaria		$30/case
Underlying assumptions for table A1.5—Intermittent preventive treatment of malaria		
Total female population in high-transmission area (this changes every year proportional to population growth, that is, by 3 percent)	2,500,000 in 2005	
Proportion of women at childbearing age in stable (high) transmission areas	44 percent	
Percent of pregnant women to receive two doses of intermittent preventive treatment with sulphadoxine-pyrimethamine	5 percent	
Percentage of those pregnant who may be HIV positive to receive a monthly dose of sulphadoxine-pyrimethamine	5 percent	
Underlying assumptions for table A1.5—Diagnosis		
Proportion of cases to be diagnosed at health services with laboratory facilities	30 percent of cases	$0.40/case diagnosed
Microscopes provided to hospitals and district health centers	3 microscopes/district	$2,120/microscope
Rapid diagnostic tests to be used at peripheral health facilities where there is no microscopy and at the community level	70 percent of clinical episodes	$0.61/rapid diagnostic test kit

Description	Assumption	Unit or value
Table A1.12		
Underlying assumptions for calculating requirements for malaria prevention and control in Ethiopia (organized by table) *(continued)*		
Underlying assumptions for table A1.6—Long-lasting insecticidal bednets		
Long-lasting insecticidal bednets		$5/net
Cost of handling and distribution of long-lasting insecticidal bednets		$2/net
All future bednets will be long-lasting insecticidal bednets		
Target to scale up insecticide-treated bednets	Increase from a target of 45 percent coverage with insecticide-treated bednets in 2005 to 100 percent coverage by 2007 and maintain 100 percent coverage until 2015 for all people living in malarious areas	
At-risk population eligible for insecticide-treated bednets	30 percent of at-risk population	
Coverage for following year	Those without insecticide-treated bednets in preceding year plus new population at risk added because of population growth	
Total number of households	Total population at risk divided by 5	
Long-lasting insecticidal bednets per household	3 long-lasting insecticidal bednets per household	
Frequency of replacement of long-lasting insecticide-treated bednets	Replacement every four years (bednets distributed in 2004 will be replaced by 2008, bednets of 2005 will be replaced by 2009, and so on)	
Underlying assumptions for table A1.6—Indoor residual spraying and larviciding		
Total price of insecticide		$5/kg of insecticide
Cost of indoor residual spraying is fully covered by the government; however, because of financial constraints, coverage with indoor residual spraying is limited to only about 25 percent of epidemic-prone areas		
At-risk population protected by indoor residual spraying	60 percent of at-risk population	
Number of households to be sprayed	Total population at risk eligible for indoor residual spraying, divided by 5	
Sprayable surface area per household	About 120 m^2 on average	
Amount of insecticide (DDT) required	Total surface area to be sprayed multiplied by required standard dosage of 2.67 gm/m^2 with 10 percent safety margins	
Indoor residual spraying cycle	30 working days/year	
One spray person sprays 360 units in one cycle	At 12 unit structures/day	
Total spray persons needed	Total number of unit structures targeted to be sprayed divided by an output of one spray person (12 unit structures per person per day x 30 working days)	
Total spray days	46 days (30 working days + 10 market and Sundays + 6 training days)	

Table A1.12

Underlying assumptions for calculating requirements for malaria prevention and control in Ethiopia (organized by table)

(continued)

Description	Assumption	Unit or value
Personnel	5-person squads of spray people	
One spray team	5 squads per team	
Field equipment such as tents and fly tents	One tent for each squad, team leader, and supervisor and multiplied by total number of squads, teams, and supervisors	
Safety protection materials such as coveralls, huts, hand gloves, goggles, buckets, soap, and so on, calculated for each spray person, squad chief, team leader, and supervisor		
Underlying assumptions for table A1.8—Health extension package and refresher training of existing health workers		
A total of 30,000 health extension workers will receive training for 8 days on malaria prevention and control through 2009; thereafter, through 2015, an estimated 1,000 health extension workers will be trained each year		$10/day
A total of 150,000 community health workers and community health promoters will receive training for 8 days on malaria prevention and control through 2009; thereafter, through 2015, an estimated 5,000 community health workers and community health promoters will be trained each year		$10/day
Provision of one motorcycle to each health extension worker is assumed through 2009; thereafter, a replacement for 25 percent of the motorcycles is assumed through 2015.		$5,000/ motorcycle
Health extension workers, community health workers, and community health promoters are first-level service providers at community level		
Two health extension workers, 5 community health workers, and 5 community health promoters would be assigned for a village of 5,000 people		
Underlying assumptions for table A1.10—Program management		
Two trucks and three pickups per district are required to transport spray equipment, insecticide supervisory personnel, and so on		
15 percent spare parts and maintenance and 25 percent replenishment is considered every 5 years		

Notes

Chapter 1

1. Transmitted from person to person through the bite of a female *Anopheles* mosquito, malaria is an infection of red blood cells in human populations caused by protozoa of the genus *Plasmodium*. Four species of *Plasmodium* infect humans: *Plasmodium falciparum, P. vivax, P. malariae,* and *P. ovale.* Of these four species, *P. falciparum* infection is the main cause of mortality from malaria throughout the tropics and subtropics, especially in tropical Africa (Snow and Gilles 2002). Only about 10–20 percent of the world's cases of *P. vivax* infection occur in Africa, south of the Sahara, with significantly low incidences across the central belt of this continent due to the Duffy negative trait (Mendis and others 2001).

2. The other founding partners of Roll Back Malaria include the World Bank, the United Nations Children's Fund, and the United Nations Development Programme. Since its inception, more than 90 multilateral, bilateral, nongovernmental, and private sector organizations have become actively engaged with the initiative.

3. All dollar amounts are U.S. dollars unless otherwise indicated.

Chapter 2

1. Trape and his colleagues (1998) reported that the emergence and development of chloroquine resistance resulted in a 2.1- to 5.5-fold increase in mortality risk among children 0–9 years old in several populations in the Sahel.

Chapter 4

1. HRP2 is a water soluble protein produced by asexual stages and young gametocytes of *P. falciparum.*

2. pLDH is a soluble glycolytic enzyme produced by sexual and asexual states of all four *Plasmodium* parasites infecting humans.

Chapter 5

1. See www.INDEPTH-Network.net for full inventory of sites.

Chapter 7

1. See www.transparency.org/ for further information.
2. For further details on the Equator Principles see www.equator-principles.com/.
3. These are available at www.theglobalfund.org/.

Chapter 8

1. See www.measuredhs.com for further information.
2. See www.childinfo.org for further information.

Chapter 9

1. See www.ipti-malaria.org for further information.
2. *Sporozoite* is the parasite stage that is transmitted from mosquitoes to people.
3. *Merozoite* is the parasite stage that is initially released from the infected liver ce
and rapidly invades and replicates in circulating red blood cells.

References

Alemayehu, T., T. A. Ghebreyesus, A. Bosman, K. H. Witten, and A. Teklehaimanot. 1998. "Community-Based Malaria Control Programme in Tigray Region, Northern Ethiopia: Results of a Mortality Survey of Children under 5 Years of Age Living in Rural Areas." *Ethiopian Journal of Health Development* 12: 203–11.

Alemayehu, T., Y. Ye-ebiyo, T. A. Ghebreyesus, K. H. Witten, A. Bosman, and A. Teklehaimanot. 1998. "Malaria, Schistosomiasis and Intestinal Helminths in Relation to Microdams in Tigray, Northern Ethiopia." *Parassitologia* 40: 259–67.

Alilio, M. S., A. Kitua, K. Njunwa, M. Medina, A. M. Rønn, J. Mhina, F. Msuya, J. Mahundi, J.M. Depinay, S. Whyte, A. Krasnik, and I. C. Byrgbjerg. 2004. "Malaria Control at the District Level in Africa: The Case of the Muheza District in Northeastern Tanzania." *American Journal of Tropical Medicine and Hygiene* 71 (2 suppl.): 205–13.

Alonso, P. L., J. Sacarlal, J. J. Aponte, A. Leach, E. Macete, J. Milman, I. Mandomando, B. Spiessens, C. Guinovart, M. Espasa, Q. Bassat, P. Aide, O. Ofori-Anyinam, M. M. Navia, S. Corachan, M. Ceuppens, M. C. Dubois, M. A. Demoitie, F. Dubovsky, C. Menendez, N. Tornieport, W. R. Ballou, R. Thompson, and J. Cohen. 2004. "Efficacy of the RTS,S/AS02A Vaccine Against Plasmodium falciparum Infection and Disease in Young African Children: Randomised Controlled Trial." *The Lancet* 364 (9443): 1411–20.

Amin, A. A., V. Marsh, A. M. Noor, S. A. Ochola, and R. W. Snow. 2003. "The Use of Formal and Informal Curative Services in the Management of Paediatric Fevers in Four Districts in Kenya. *Tropical Medicine and International Health* 8 (12): 1143–52.

Baird, J. 2000. "Resurgent Malaria at the Millennium: Control Strategies in Crisis." *Dru* 59 (4): 719–43.

Balfour, T. 2002. "TB and Malaria in SADC Countries." In Petrida Ijumba, ed., *African Health Review 2002*. Durban, South Africa: Health Systems Trust.

Ballou, W. R., M. Arevalo-Herrera, D. Carucci, T. L. Richie, G. Corradin, C. Γ Druilhe, B. K. Giersing, A. Saul, D. G. Heppner, K. E. Kester, D. E. Lana A. V. S. Hill, W. Pan, and J. D. Cohen. 2004. "Update on the Clinical D∈ of Candidate Malaria Vaccines." *American Journal of Tropical Medicine* 71 (2 suppl.): 239–47.

Barat, L. M., N. Palmer, S. Basu, E. Worrall, K. Hanson, and A. Mills. 2004. "Do Malaria Control Interventions Reach the Poor? A View through the Equity Lens." *American Journal of Tropical Medicine and Hygiene* 71 (2 suppl): 174–78.

Brabin, B. J., C. Romagosa, S. Abdelgalil, C. Menendez, F. H. Verhoeff, R. McGready, K. A. Fletcher, S. Owens, U. D'Alessandro, F. Nosten, P. R. Fischer, and J. Ordi. 2004. "The Sick Placenta—The Role of Malaria." *Placenta* 25 (5): 359–78.

Bradley, D. J. 2001. "The Biological and Epidemiological Basis of Global Public Goods for Health." Working Paper WG2: 15. Commission on Macroeconomics and Health. Cambridge, Mass. and Geneva. [www.cmhealth.org/docs/wg2_paper15.pdf].

Bredenkamp, B., B. L. Sharp, S. D. Mthembu, D. N. Durrheim, and K. I. Barnes. 2001. "Failure of Sulphadoxine-pyrimethamine in Treating Plasmodium falciparum Malaria in KwaZulu-Natal." *South African Medical Journal* 91 (11): 970–72.

Breman, J. 2001. "The Ears of the Hippopotamus: Manifestations, Determinant, and Estimates of the Malaria Burden." *American Journal of Tropical Medicine and Hygiene* 64: 1–11.

Bruce-Chwatt, L. J. 1988. "History of Malaria from Prehistory to Eradication." In W. H. Wernsdorfer and I. McGregor, eds., *Malaria: Principles and Practice of Malariology* Vol. 1. Edinburgh and New York: Churchill Livingstone.

Campbell, C. C., W. Chin, W. E. Collins, S. M. Teutsch, and D. M. Moss. 1979. "Chloroquine-Resistant *Plasmodium falciparum* from East Africa: Cultivation and Drug Sensitivity of the Tanzanian I/CDC Strain from an American Tourist." *The Lancet* 2 (8153): 1151–54.

Casimiro, S. 2003. "Susceptibility and Resistance to Insecticides Among Malaria Vector Mosquitoes in Mozambique." Thesis. University of KwaZulu-Natal, South Africa.

Castro, M. C., Y. Yamagata, D. Mtasiwa, M. Tanner, J. Utzinger, J. Keiser, and B. H. Singer. 2004. "Integrated Urban Malaria Control: A Case Study in Dar es Salaam, Tanzania." *American Journal of Tropical Medicine and Hygiene* 71 (2 suppl.): 103–17.

Chahnazarian, A., D. C. Ewbank, B. Makani, and K. Ekouevi. 1993. "Impact of Selective Primary Care on Childhood Mortality in a Rural Health Zone of Zaire." *International Journal of Epidemiology* 22 (1 suppl.): 32–41.

Chandre, F., F. Darrier, L. Manga, M. Akogbeto, O. Faye, J. Mouchet, and P. Guillet. 1999. "Status of Pyrethroid Resistance in Anopheles Gambiae Sensu Lato." *Bulletin of the World Health Organization* 77 (3): 230–34.

Comoro, C., Nsimba, S. E. D., Warsame, M., and Tomson, G. 2003. "Local Understanding, Perceptions and Reported Practices of Mothers/Guardians and Health Workers on Childhood Malaria in a Tanzanian District—Implications for Malaria Control." *Acta Tropica* 87 (3): 305–13.

Connor, S., M. Thomson, and D. H. Molyneux. 1999. "Forecasting and Prevention of Epidemic Malaria: New Perspectives on an Old Problem." *Parassitologia* 41 (1–3): 439–48.

Conteh, L., B. L. Sharp, E. Streat, A. Barreto, and S. Konar. 2004. "The Cost and Cost Effectiveness of Malaria Vector Control by Residual Insecticide House-Spraying in Southern Mozambique: a Rural and Urban Analysis." *Tropical Medicine and International Health* 9 (1): 125–32.

Copenhagen Consensus. 2004. "Copenhagen Consensus: The Results." [Retrieved on August 10, 2004, from www.copenhagenconsensus.com].

Cox, J., M. H. Craig, D. Le Sueur, and B. Sharp. 1999. *Mapping Malaria Risk in the Highlands of Africa.* MARA/HIMAL Technical Report. Durban, South Africa.

Curtis, C. F. 2002a. "Restoration of Malaria Control in the Madagascar Highlands by DDT Spraying." Comment. *American Journal of Tropical Medicine and Hygiene* 66 (1): 1.

———. 2002b. "Should the Use of DDT Be Revived for Malaria Vector Control?" *Bio Medica* 22 (4): 455–61.

Curtis, C. F., and A. E. Mnzava. 2000. "Comparison of House Spraying and Insecticide-Treated Nets for Malaria Control." Comment. *Bulletin of the World Health Organization* 78 (12): 1389–1400.

Curtis, C., C. Maxwell, M. Lemnge, W. L. Kilama, R. W. Steketee, W. A. Hawley, Y. Bergevin, C. C. Campbell, J. Sachs, A. Teklehaimano, S. Ochola, H. Guyatt, and R. W. Snow. 2003. "Scaling-up Coverage with Insecticide-Treated Nets Against Malaria in Africa: Who Should Pay?" *Lancet Infectious Diseases* 3 (5): 304–7.

De Plaen, R., M. L. Seka, and A. Koutoua, 2004. "The Paddy, the Vector and the Caregiver: Lessons From an Ecosystem Approach to Irrigation and Malaria in Northern Côte d'Ivoire." *Acta Tropica* 89 (2): 135–46.

De Savigny, D., H. Kasale, C. Mbuya, and G. Reid. 2004. *Fixing Health Systems.* Ottawa: International Development Research Center.

De Savigny, D., and F. Binka. 2004. "Monitoring Future Impact on Malaria Burden in Sub-Saharan Africa." *American Journal of Tropical Medicine and Hygiene* 71(2 suppl), 224–31.

Deming, M. S., A. Gayibor, K. Murphy, T. S. Jones, and T. Karsa. 1989. "Home Treatment of Febrile Children with Antimalarial Drugs in Togo." *Bulletin of the World Health Organization* 67: 695–700.

Deressam, W., A. Ali, and F. Enqusellassie. 2003. "Self-Treatment of Malaria in Rural Communities, Butajira, Southern Ethiopia." *Bulletin of the World Health Organization* 81 (4): 261–68.

Diallo, A. B., G. De Serres, A. H. Beavogui, C. Lapointe, and P. Viens. 2001. "Home Care of Malaria-Infected Children of Less Than 5 Years of Age in a Rural Area of the Republic of Guinea." *Bulletin of the World Health Organization* 79 (1) 28–32.

Ettling, M., D. A. McFarland, L. J. Schultz, and L. Chitsulo. 1994. "Economic Impact of Malaria in Malawian Households." *Tropical Medicine and Parasitology* 45 (1): 74–79.

Fontaine, R., A. E. Najjar, and J. S. Prince. 1961. "The 1958 Malaria Epidemic in Ethiopia." *American Journal of Tropical Medicine and Hygiene* 10: 795–803.

Gallup, J., and J. Sachs. 2001. "The Economic Burden of Malaria." *American Journal of Tropical Medicine and Hygiene* 64 (90010): 85–96.

Gamage-Mendis, A. C., R. Carter, C. Mendis, A. P. De Zoysa, P. R. Herath, and K. N. Mendis. 1991. "Clustering of Malaria Infections within an Endemic Population: Risk of Malaria Associated with the Type of Housing Construction." *American Journal of Tropical Medicine and Hygiene* 45 (1): 77–85.

Gardner, M. J., N. Hall, E. Fung, O. White, M. Berriman, R. W. Hyman, J. M. Carlton, A. Pain, K. E. Nelson, S. Bowman, I. T. Paulsen, K. James, J. A. Eisen, K. Rutherford, S. L. Salzberg, A. Craig, S. Kyes, M. S. Chan, V. Nene, S. J. Shallom, B. Suh, J. Peterson, S. Angiuoli, M. Pertea, J. Allen, J. Selengu, D. Haft, M. W. Mather, A. B. Vaidya, D. M. Martin, A. H. Fairlamb, M. J. Fraunholz, D. S. Roos, S. A. Ralph, G. I. McFadden, L. M. Cummings, G. M. Subramanian, C. Mungall, J. C. Venter, D. J. Carucci, S. L. Hoffman, C. Newbold, R. W. Davis, C. M. Fraser, and B. Barrell. 2002. "Genome Sequence of the Human Malaria Parasite Plasmodium falciparum." *Nature* 419 (6906): 498–511.

Garg, M., N. Gopinathan, P. Bodhe, and N. A. Kshirsagar. 1995. "Vivax Malaria Resistant to Choloroquine: Case Reports from Bombay." *Transactions of Royal Society Tropical Medicine and Hygiene* 89: 656–57.

GFATM (Global Fund to Fight AIDS, Tuberculosis and Malaria). 2004a. "GFATM ress Reports." [Retrieved on May 26, 2004, from www.theglobalfund.org/e raised/reports/].

———. 2004b. "Global Fund Commitments to Improve International M ment." [Retrieved October 27, 2004, from www.theglobalfund.org/ globalfund_commitments1.pdf].

Ghebreyesus, T. A., T. Alemayehu, A. Bosman, K. H. Witten, and A. Teklehaimanot. 1996. "Community Participation in Malaria Control in Tigray Region Ethiopia." *Acta Tropica* 61 (2): 145–56.

Ghosh, A. K., L. A. Moreira, and M. Jacobs-Lorena. 2002. "Plasmodium-Mosquito Interactions, Phage Display Libraries and Transgenic Mosquitoes Impaired for Malaria Transmission." *Insect Biochemistry and Molecular Biology* 32 (10): 1325–31.

Girardin, O., D. Dao, B. G. Koudou, C. Esse, G. Cisse, T. Yao, E. K. N'Goran, A. B. Tschannen, G. Bordmann, B. Lehmann, C. Nsabimana, J. Keiser, G. F. Killeen, B H. Singer, M. Tanner, and J. Utzinger. 2004. "Opportunities and Limiting Factors of Intensive Vegetable Farming in Malaria Endemic Côte d'Ivoire." *Acta Tropica* 89 (2): 109–23.

Gladwell, M. 2002. "Fred Soper and the Global Malaria Eradication Programme." *Journal of Public Health Policy* 23 (4): 479–97.

Graves, P. M. 2004. *Eritrea: Malaria Surveillance, Epidemic Preparedness, and Control Program Strengthening.* Washington, D.C.: Environmental Health Project.

Greenwood, B., and T. Mutabingwa. 2002. "Malaria in 2002." *Nature* 415 (6872): 670–72.

Guerin, P. J., P. Olliaro, F. Nosten, P. Druilhe, R. Laxminarayan, F. Binka, W. L. Kilama N. Ford, N. J. White. 2002. "Malaria: Current Status of Control, Diagnosis, Treatment, and a Proposed Agenda for Research and Development." *Lancet Infectious Diseases* 2 (9): 564–73.

Gunawardena, D., A. Wickremasinghe, L. Muthuwatta, S. Weerasingha, J. Rajakaruna, T. Senanayaka, P. K. Kotta, N. Attanayake, R. Carter, and K. N. Mendis. 1998. "Malaria Risk Factors in an Endemic Region of Sri Lanka, and the Impact and Cost Implications of Risk Factor-Based Interventions." *American Journal of Tropical Medicine and Hygiene* 58 (5): 533–42.

Gwatkin, D. R., and M. Guillot. 1999. *The Burden of Disease among the World's Poor: Current Situation, Future Trends, and Implications for Strategy.* Washington, D.C.: World Bank and Global Forum for Health Research.

Hargreaves, K., L. L. Koekemoer, B. D. Brooke, R. H. Hunt, J. Mthembu, and M. Coetzee. 2000. "Anopheles funestus Resistant to Pyrethroid Insecticides in South Africa." *Medical and Veterinary Entomology* 14 (2): 181–89.

Hoek, W. 2004. "How Can Better Farming Methods Reduce Malaria?" *Acta Tropica* 89 (2): 95–97.

IDRC (International Development Research Centre)/TEHIP (Tanzania Essential Health Interventions Project). 2004. "Origins of TEHIP." [Retrieved on September 21, 2004 from http://web.idrc.ca/en/ev-3231-201-1-DO_TOPIC.html].

INDEPTH Network. Website. www.INDEPTH-Network.net.

Institute of Medicine. 2004. *Saving Lives, Buying Time: Economics of Malaria Drugs in an Age of Resistance.* Washington, D.C.: National Academies Press.

IPTi (Intermittent Preventive Treatment in Infants) Consortium. Website. www.ipti malaria.org/.

Jacob, B. G., J. L. Regens, C. M. Mbogo, A. K. Githeko, J. Keating, C. M. Swalm, J. T Gunter, J. I. Githure, and J. C. Beier. 2003. "Occurrence and Distribution of Anopheles (Diptera: Culicidae) Larval Habitats on Land Cover Change Sites in Urban Kisumu and Urban Malindi, Kenya." *Journal of Medical Entomology* 40 (6): 777–84.

Joncour, G. 1956. "La Lutte Contre le Paludisme a Madagascar." *Bulletin of the World Health Organization* 15: 711–23.

Keiser, J., J. Utzinger, Z. Premji, Y. Yamagata, and B. H. Singer. 2002. "Acridine Orange for Malaria Diagnosis: Its Diagnostic Performance, Its Promotion and Implementation in Tanzania, and the Implications for Malaria Control." *Annals of Tropical Medicine and Parasitology* 96 (7): 643–54.

Khaemba, B. M., A. Mutani, and M. K. Bett. 1994. "Studies of Anopheline Mosquitoes Transmitting Malaria in a Newly Developed Highland Urban Area: a Case Study of Moi University and Its Environs." *East African Medical Journal* 71 (3): 159–64.

Kidane, G., and R. H. Morrow. 2000. "Teaching Mothers to Provide Home Treatment of Malaria in Tigray, Ethiopia: A Randomised Trial." *The Lancet* 356 (9229): 550–55.

Kiszewski, A., and A. Teklehaimanot. 2004. "A Review of the Clinical and Epidemiological Burdens of Epidemic Malaria." *American Journal of Tropical Medicine and Hygiene* 71 (2 suppl.): 128–35.

Kofoed, P. E., A. Rodrigues, F. Co, K. Hedegaard, L. Rombo, and P. Aaby. 2004. "Which Children Come to the Health Centre for Treatment of Malaria?" *Acta Tropica* 90 (1): 17–22.

Konradsen, F., P. Amerasinghe, W. Van der Hoek, F. Amerasinghe, D. Perera, and M. Piyaratne. 2003. "Strong Association Between House Characteristics and Malaria Vectors in Sri Lanka." *American Journal of Tropical Medicine and Hygiene* 68 (2): 177–81.

Korenromp, E. L., B. G. Williams, E. Gouws, C. Dye, and R. W. Snow. 2003. "Measurement of Trends in Childhood Malaria Mortality in Africa: An Assessment of Progress toward Targets Based on Verbal Autopsy." *Lancet Infectious Diseases* 3 (6): 349–58.

Kyaw, M. P., M. Oo, M. Lwin, A. K. H. Thawzin, and N.N. Yin. 1993. "Emergence of Chloroquine-resistant Plasmodium vivax in Myanmar (Burma)." *Transactions of Royal Society of Tropical Medicine and Hygiene* 87: 687.

Lengeler, C. 1998. "Insecticide Treated Bednets and Curtains for Malaria Control." In *The Cochrane Library* (Vol. 3). Oxford: Update Software.

Lepers, J. P., P. Deloron, M. D. Andriamagatiana-Rason, J. A. Ramanamirija, and P. Coulanges. 1990. "Newly Transmitted Plasmodium falciparum Malaria in the Central Highland Plateaux of Madagascar: Assessment of Clinical Impact in a Rural Community." *Bulletin of the World Health Organization* 68 (2): 217–22.

Liang, K. C. 1991. "Historical Review of Malaria Control Program in Taiwan." *Kao-Hsiung i Hsueh Ko Hsueh Tsa Chih (Kaohsiung Journal of Medical Sciences)* 7 (5): 271–277.

Lindblade, K. A., T. P. Eisele, J. E. Gimnig, J. A. Alaii, F. Odhiambo, F. O. ter Kuile, W. A. Hawley, K. A. Wannemuehler, A., P. A. Phillips-Howard, D. H. Rosen, B. L. Nahlem, D. J. Terlouw, K. Adazu, J. M. Vulule, and L. Slutsker. 2004. "Sustainability of Reductions in Malaria Transmission and Infant Mortality in Western Kenya with Use of Insecticide-Treated Bednets: 4 to 6 years of Follow-up." Comment. *Journal of the American Medical Association* 291 (21): 2571–80.

Lindsay, S. W., M. Jawara, K. Paine, M. Pinder, G. E. L. Walraven, and P. M Emerson. 2003. "Changes in House Design Reduce Exposure to Malaria Mosquitoes." *Tropical Medicine and International Health* 8 (6): 512–17.

Litsios, S. 1996. *The Tomorrow of Malaria*. Karori, New Zealand: Pacific Press.

LSDI (Lumbobo Spatial Development Initiative). Website. www.malaria.org.za/lsdi/Overview/overview.html.

Lu, B. 1988. "Environmental Management for the Control of Rice-field Breeding Mosquitoes in China." In *Vector-Borne Disease Control in Humans Through Rice Agroecosystem Management: Proceedings of the Workshop on Research and Training Needs in the Field of Integrated Vector-Borne Disease Control in Riceland Agroecosystems of Developing Countries*. Manila: International Rice Research Institute in collaboration with the World Health Organization/Food and Agriculture Organization of the United Nations/United National Environmental Programme Panel of Experts on Environmental Management for Vector Control.

Magesa, S. M., T. J. Wilkes, A. E. Mnzava, K. J. Njunwa, J. Myamba, M. D. Kivuyo, N. Hill, J. D. Lines, C. F. Curtis. 1991. "Trial of Pyrethroid Impregnated Bednets in an Area of Tanzania Holoendemic for Malaria. Part 2. Effects on the Malaria Vector Population." *Acta Tropica* 49 (2): 97–108.

Makler, M. T., C. J. Palmer, and A. L. Ager. 1998. "A Review of Practical Technique for the Diagnosis of Malaria." *Annals of Tropical Medicine and Parasitology* 92 (4) 419–433.

Marques, A. C. 1987. "Human Migration and the Spread of Malaria in Brazil." *Paras, tology Today* 3: 166–70.

Massaga, J. J., A. Y. Kitua, M. M. Lemnge, J. A. Akida, L. N. Malle, A. M. Ronn, T. C Theander, I. C. Bygbjerg. 2003. "Effect of Intermittent Treatment with Amodiaquin on Anaemia and Malarial Fevers in Infants in Tanzania: A Randomised Placebo-Cor trolled Trial." *The Lancet* 361 (9372): 1853–60.

Maxwell, C. A., W. Chambo, M. Mwaimu, F. Magogo, I. A. Carneiro, and C. F. Curti 2003. "Variation of Malaria Transmission and Morbidity with Altitude in Tar zania and with Introduction of Alphacypermethrin Treated Nets." *Malaria Journ* 2 (1): 28.

Maxwell, C. A., E. Msuya, M. Sudi, K. J. Njunwa, I. A. Carneiro, and C. F. Curtis. 200: "Effect of Community-Wide Use of Insecticide-treated Nets for 3–4 Years on Malari Morbidity in Tanzania." *Tropical Medicine and International Health* 7 (12): 1003–0₈

Mayhew, S. 1996. "Integrating MCH/FP and STD/HIV Services: Current Debates an Future Directions." Health Policy and Planning 11 (4): 339–53.

McCombie, S. C. 1996. "Treatment Seeking for Malaria: A Review of Recent Research *Social Science and Medicine* 43 (6): 933–45.

Mendis, K., B. J. Sina, P. Marchesini, and R. Carter. 2001. "The Neglected Burden Plasmodium vivax Malaria." *American Journal of Tropical Medicine and Hygiene* 6 (1–2 suppl.): 97–106.

Menendez, C. 1995. "Malaria During Pregnancy: a Priority Area of Malaria Research a₌ Control." *Parasitology Today* 11: 178–83.

Mills, A., and S. Shillcutt. 2004a. Personal communication, received August 9, 2004.

———. 2004b. "Copenhagen Consensus Challenge Paper on Communicable Disease: [www.copenhagenconsensus.com/files/filer/cc/papers/communicable_disease 160404.pdf].

MIM (Multilateral Initiative for Malaria). 2001. *Research Capability Strengthening.* Genev TDR Task Force.

MMV (Medicines for Malaria Venture). Website. www.mmv.org.

———. 2003. "Curing Malaria Together." Geneva.

Moerman, F., C. Lengeler, J. Chimumbwa, A. Talisuna, A. Erhart, M. Coosemans, a₌ U. D'Alessandro. 2003. "The Contribution of Health-care Services to a Sound a₌ Sustainable Malaria-control Policy." *Lancet Infectious Diseases* 3 (2): 99–102.

Molyneux, D. H. 1998. "Vector-borne Parasitic Diseases—an Overview of Rece Changes." *International Journal for Parasitology* 28: 927–34.

Molyneux, D. H., and V. M. Nantulya, 2004. "Linking Disease Control Programmes Rural Africa: A Pro-poor Strategy to Reach Abuja Targets and Millennium Develo ment Goals." *British Medical Journal* 328 (7448): 1129–32.

Moody, A. 2002. "Rapid Diagnostic Tests for Malaria Parasites." *Clinical Microbiol₌ Reviews* 15 (1): 66–78.

Moore, S., E. G. Surgey, , and M. Cadwgan. 2002. "Malaria Vaccines: Where Are We a₌ Where Are We Going?" *Lancet Infectious Diseases* 2 (12): 737–43. Erratum in *Lam Infectious Diseases* (10) 673.

Moorthy, V. S., M. F. Good, and A. V. Hill. 2004. "Malaria Vaccine Developments." *7 Lancet* 363 (9403): 150–56.

MSF (Médecins Sans Frontières). 2003. "KwaZulu-Natal—Province-Wide Impleme tation of ACT." [Retrieved on August 3, 2004, from www.msf.org/content/pa₌ cfm?articleid=C97460A4-D210-448C-B69000F20748ED0D].

Murphy, G. S., H. Basri, E. M. Andersen, M. J. Bangs, J. Gorden, and others. 1993. "Vivax Malaria Resistant to Treatment and Prophylaxis with Chloroquine." *The Lancet* 341 (8837): 96–100.

Murphy, S., and J. Breman. 2001. "Gaps in the Childhood Malaria Burden in Africa: Cerebral Malaria, Neurological Sequelae, Anemia, Respiratory Distress, Hypoglycemia, and Complications of Pregnancy." *American Journal of Tropical Medicine and Hygiene* 64 (90010): 57–67.

Murray, C. K., D. Bell, R. A. Gasser, and C. Wongsrichanalai. 2003. "Rapid Diagnostic Testing for Malaria." *Tropical Medicine and International Health* 8 (10): 876–83.

Musawenkosi, L. H. M., B. Sharp, and C. Lengeler. 2004. "Historical Review of Malarial Control in Southern Africa with Emphasis on the Use of Indoor Residual House-Spraying." *Tropical Medicine and International Health* 9 (8): 846–56.

Mutero, C. M., C. Kabutha, V. Kimani, L. Kabuage, G. Gitau, J. Ssennyonga, J. Githure, L. Muthami, A. Kaida, L. Musyoka, E. Kiarie, and M. Oganda. 2004. "A Transdisciplinary Perspective on the Links Between Malaria and Agroecosystems in Kenya." *Acta Tropica* 89 (2): 171–86.

Mwenesi, H., T. Harpham, and R. W. Snow. 1995. "Child Malaria Treatment Practices among Mothers in Kenya." *Social Science and Medicine* 40 (9): 1271–77.

Nájera, J. A., B. H. Liese, and J. Hammer. 1992. *Malaria: New Patterns and Perspectives.* Washington, D.C.: World Bank.

N'Guessan, R., F. Darriet, P. Guillet, P. Carnevale, M. Traore-Lamizana, V. Corbel, A. A. Koffi, and F. Chandre. 2003. "Resistance to Carbosulfan in Anopheles gambiae from Ivory Coast, Based on Reduced Sensitivity of Acetylcholinesterase." *Medical and Veterinary Entomology* 17 (1): 19–25.

Nguyen-Dinh, P., I. K. Schwartz, J. D. Sexton, B. Egumb, B. Bolange, K. Ruti, N. Nkuku-Pela, and M. Wery. 1985. "In Vivo and In Vitro Susceptibility to Chloroquine of Plasmodium falciparum in Kinshasa and Mbuji-Mayi, Zaire." *Bulletin of the World Health Organization* 63 (2): 325–30.

Nigatu, W., M. Abebe, and A. Dejene. 1992. *"Plasmodium vivax* and *P. falciparum* Epidemiology in Gambella, South-west Ethiopia." *Tropical Medicine and Parasitology* 43 (3): 181–85.

Njama, D. G., Dorsey, D. Guwatudde, K. Kigonya, B. Greenhouse, S. Musisi, and M. R. Kamya. 2003. "Urban Malaria: Primary Caregivers' Knowledge, Attitudes, Practices and Predictors of Malaria Incidence in a Cohort of Ugandan Children." *Tropical Medicine and International Health* 8 (8): 685–92.

Nosten, F., and P. Brasseur. 2002. "Combination Therapy for Malaria: the Way Forward?" *Drugs* 62 (9): 1315–29.

Nosten, F., S. Rogerson, J. Beeson, R. McGready, T. Mutabingwa, and B. Brabin. 2004. "Malaria in Pregnancy and the Endemicity Spectrum: What Can We Learn?" *Trends in Parasitology* 20 (9): 425–32.

Oaks, S. C., V.S. Mitchell, G. W. Pearson, and C. C. J. Carpenter, eds. 1991. *Malaria: Obstacles and Opportunities.* Washington, D.C.: National Academies Press.

Pagnoni, F., N. Convelbo, J. Tiendrebeogo, S. Cousens, and F. Esposito. 1997. "A Community-Based Programme to Provide Prompt and Adequate Treatment of Presumptive Malaria in Children." *Transactions of the Royal Society of Tropical Medicine and Hygiene* 91 (5): 512–17.

Parise, M., J. Ayisi, B. Nahlen, L. Schultz, J. Roberts, A. Misore, R. Muga, A. J. Oloo, and R. W. Steketee. 1998. "Efficacy of Sulfadoxine-pyrimethamine for Prevention of Placental Malaria in an Area of Kenya with a High Prevalence of Malaria and Human Immunodeficiency Virus Infection." *American Journal of Tropical Medicine and Hygiene* 59 (5): 813–22.

Patz, J. A., T. K. Graczyk, N. Geller, and A. Y. Vittor. 2000. "Effects of Environmental Change on Emerging Parasitic Diseases." *International Journal for Parasitology* 30 (12–13): 1395–1405.

Phillips, E. J., J. S. Keystone, and K. C. Kain. 1996. "Failure of Combined Chloroquine and High Dose Primaquine Therapy for *Plasmodium vivax* Malaria Acquired in Guyana, South America." *Clinical Infectious Diseases* 23: 1171–1173.

Pietra, V., R. Jambou, D. Rakotondramarina, J. L. Sahondra-Harisoa, I. Jeanne, and D. Modiano. 2002. "Le Paludisme sur les Hautes Terres Centrales de Madagascar." In P. Mauclère, ed., *Atlas évolutif du Paludisme à Madagascar 2002*. Antananarivo: Institut Pasteur de Madagascar.

Pukrittayakamee, S., M. Imwong, S. Looareesuwan, and N. J. White. 2004. "Therapeutic Responses to Antimalarial and Antibacterial Drugs in Vivax Malaria." *Acta Tropica* 8 (3): 351–56.

Randrianarivelojosia, M. 2004. "Malaria Control Strategy in Madagascar." (E-mail communication).

RBM (Roll Back Malaria). 2004. "Facts on ACTs: An Update on Recent Progress in Policy and Access to Treatment." [Retrieved on July 9, 2004, from http://rbm.who.int/cmc_upload/0/000/015/364/RBMInfosheet_9.htm].

Richie, T. L., and A. Saul. 2002. "Progress and Challenges for Malaria Vaccines." *Nature* 415 (7): 694–701.

Rieckmann, K. H., D. R. Davis, and D. C. Hutton. 1989. "*Plasmodium vivax* Resistance to Chloroquine?" *The Lancet* 334 (8673): 1183–84.

Roberts, D. R., S. Manguin, and J. Mouchet. 2000. "DDT House Spraying and Re-Emerging Malaria." Comment. *The Lancet* 356 (9226): 330–32.

Romi, R., M. C. Razaiarimanga, R. Raharimanga, E. M. Rakotondraibe, L. H. Ranaivo, V. Pietra, A. Raveloson, and G. Majori. 2002. "Impact of the Malaria Control Campaign (1993–1998) in the Highlands of Madagascar: Parasitological and Entomological Data." *American Journal of Tropical Medicine and Hygiene* 66 (1): 2–6.

Rosen, J. B., and J. G. Breman. 2004. "Malaria Intermittent Preventive Treatment in Infants, Chemoprophylaxis, and Childhood Vaccinations." *The Lancet* 363 (9418): 1386–88.

Ruebush, T. K., M. K. Kern, C. C. Campbell, and A. J. Oloo. 1995. "Self-Treatment of Malaria in a Rural Area of Western Kenya." *Bulletin of the World Health Organization* 73: 229–36.

Sachs, J., and P. Malaney. 2002. "The Economic and Social Burden of Malaria." *Nature* 415 (6872): 680–685.

Schapira, A. 2002. "Determinants of Malaria in Oceania and East Asia." In E. A. Casman and H. Dowlatabadi, eds., *The Contextual Determinants of Malaria*. Washington, D.C.: Resources for the Future.

Schellenberg, D., C. Menendez, E. Kahigwa, J. Aponte, J. Vidal, M. Tanner, H. Mshinda, and P. Alonso. 2001. "Intermittent Treatment for Malaria and Anaemia Control at Time of Routine Vaccinations in Tanzanian Infants: a Randomised, Placebo-Controlled Trial." *The Lancet* 357 (9267): 1471–77.

Shankar, A. 2000. "Nutritional Modulation of Malaria Morbidity and Mortality." *Journal of Infectious Diseases* 182 (1 suppl.): 37–53.

Sharma, S. K., S. Jalees, K. Kumar, and S. J. Rahman. 1993. "Knowledge, Attitude and Beliefs about Malaria in a Tribal Area of Bastar District (Madhya Pradesh)." *Indian Journal of Public Health* 37 (4): 129–32.

Sharma, V. P. 1999. "Current Scenario of Malaria in India." *Parassitologia* 41 (1–3): 349–53.

———. 2002. "Determinants of Malaria in South Asia." In E. A. Casman and H. Dowlatabadi, eds., *The Contextual Determinants of Malaria*. Washington, D.C.: Resource for the Future.

Shepard, D. S., M. B. Ettling, U. Brinkmann, and R. Sauerborn. 1991. "The Economic Cost of Malaria in Africa." *Tropical Medicine and Parasitology* 42 (3): 199–203.

Shiffman, J., T. Beer, and Y. Wu. 2002. "The Emergence of Global Disease Control Priorities." *Health Policy and Planning* 17: 227–34.

Sibley, C. H., J. E. Hyde, P. F. G. Sims, C. V. Plowe, J. G. Kublin, E. K. Mberu, A. F. Cowman, P. A. Winstanley, W. M. Watkins, and A. M. Nzila. 2001. "Pyrimethamine-sulfadoxine Resistance in Plasmodium falciparum: What Next?" *Trends in Parasitology* 12: 582–88.

Singh, O., P. K. Raghavendra, N. Nanda, P. K. Mittal, and S. K. Subbarao. 2002. "Pyrethroid Resistance in *Anopheles culicifacies* in Surat District, Gujarat, West India." *Current Science* 82 (5): 547–50.

Singhanetra-Renard, A. 1986. "Population Movement, Socio-economic Behavior and the Transmission of Malaria in Northern Thailand." *Southeast Asian Journal of Tropical Medicine and Public Health* 17 (3): 396–405.

Sinton, J. A. 1935. "What Malaria Costs India, Nationally, Socially and Economically." *Records of the Malaria Survey of India* 5: 223–64 and 413–89.

———. 1936. "What Malaria Costs India, Nationally, Socially and Economically." *Records of the Malaria Survey of India* 6: 91–169.

Sissoko, M. S., A. Dicko, O. J. T. Briet, M. Sissoko, I. Sagara, H. D. Keita, M. Sogoba, C. Rogier, Y. T. Toure, and O. K. Doumbo. 2004. "Malaria Incidence in Relation to Rice Cultivation in the Irrigated Sahel of Mali." *Acta Tropica* 89 (2): 161–70.

Snow, R. W., E. Eckert, and A. Teklehaimanot. 2003. "Estimating the Needs for Artesunate-based Combination Therapy for Malaria Case-management in Africa." *Trends in Parasitology* 19 (8): 363–69.

Spielman, A. U., Kitron, and R. J. Pollack. 1993. "Time Limitation and the Role of Research in the Worldwide Attempt to Eradicate Malaria." *Journal of Medical Entomology* 30 (1): 6–19.

Steketee, R. W., B. L. Nahlen, M. E. Parise, and C. Menendez. 2001. "The Burden of Malaria in Pregnancy in Malaria-endemic Areas." *American Journal of Tropical Medicine and Hygiene* 64 (1–2 suppl.): 28–35.

Takken, W. 2002. "Do Insecticide-treated Bednets Have an Effect on Malaria Vectors?" *Tropical Medicine and International Health* 7 (12): 1022–30.

Takken, W., W. B. Snellen, J. P. Verhave, B. G. J. Knols, and S. Atmosoedjono. 1990. *Environmental Measures for Malaria Control in Indonesia: A Historical Review of Species Sanitation.* Wageningen Agricultural University Papers 90.7.

Tarimo, D. S., J. N. Minjas, and I. C. Bygbjerg. 2001. "Malaria Diagnosis and Treatment Under the Strategy of the Integrated Management of Childhood Illness (IMCI): Relevance of Laboratory Support from the Rapid Immunochromatographic Tests of ICT Malaria P.f/P.v and OptiMal." *Annals of Tropical Medicine and Parasitology* 95 (5): 437–444.

Teklehaimanot, A. 1986. "Chloroquine-resistant *Plasmodium falciparum* Malaria in Ethiopia." *The Lancet* 2 (8499): 127–29.

Teklehaimanot, A., and A. Bosman. 1999. "Opportunities, Problems and Perspectives for Malaria Control in Sub-Saharan Africa." *Parasitologia* 41: 335–38.

Teklehaimanot, A., and R. W. Snow. 2002. "Will the Global Fund Help Roll Back Malaria in Africa?" *The Lancet* 360: 888–89.

Teklehaimanot, H., J. Schwartz, A. Teklehaimanot, and M. Lipsitch. 2004. "Alert Threshold Algorithms and Malaria Epidemic Detection." *Emerging Infectious Diseases* 10 (7): 1220–26.

Ter Kuile, F. O., M. E. Parise, F. H. Verhoeff, V. Udhayakumar, R. D. Newman, A. M. Van Eijk, S. Rogerson, and R. W. Steketee. 2004. "The Burden of Co-Infection with

Human Immunodeficiency Virus Type 1 and Malaria in Pregnant Women in Sub Saharan Africa." *American Journal of Tropical Medicine and Hygiene* 71 (2 suppl.) 41–54.

Thomson, M., and S. Connor. 2001. "The Development of Malaria Early Warning Sys tems for Africa." *Trends in Parasitology* 17 (9): 438–45.

Trape, J. F., G. Pison, M. P. Preziosi, C. Enel, A. Desgrees du Lou, V. Delaunay, B. Saml E. Lagarde, J. F. Molez, and F. Simondon. 1998. "Impact of Chloroquine Resistanc on Malaria Mortality." *Comptes Rendus de L'Academie des Sciences—Serie III, Scienc de la Vie* 321 (8): 689–97.

Trigg, P. I., and A. V. Kondrachine. 1998. "Commentary: Malaria Control in the 1990s *Bulletin of the World Health Organization* 76 (1): 11–16.

UNEP (United Nations Environment Programme). 2004. "Stockholm Convention on Pe sistent Organic Pollutants." [www.pops.int/documents/convtext/convtext_en.pdf].

UN Millennium Project. 2005. *Investing in Development: A Practical Plan to Achieve th Millennium Development Goals.* New York.

Utzinger, J., Y. Tozan, and B. H. Singer. 2001. "Efficacy and Cost-Effectiveness of Env ronmental Management for Malaria Control." *Tropical Medicine and Internation Health* 6: 677–87.

Utzinger, J., Y. Tozan, F. Doumani, and B. H. Singer. 2002. "The Economic Payoffs Integrated Malaria Control in the Zambian Copperbelt Between 1930 and 1950 *Tropical Medicine and International Health* 7 (8): 657–77.

Watson, M. 1921. *The Prevention of Malaria in the Federated Malay States: A Record of t Twenty Years of Progress.* London: John Murray and Sons.

Webster, D., and Hill, A. V. 2003. "Progress with New Malaria Vaccines." *Bulletin of t World Health Organization* 81 (12): 902–09.

WHO (World Health Organization). 1993. *Implementation of the Global Malaria Cont Strategy. Report of a WHO Study Group on the Implementation of the Global Plan Action for Malaria Control 1993–2000.* Geneva.

———. 1998. "Roll Back Malaria: a Global Partnership." Geneva.

———. 1999. "The Community-based Malaria Control Programme in Tigray, Northe Ethiopia: A Review of Programme Set-up, Activities, Outcomes and Impac Geneva

———. 2000a. "New Perspectives Malaria Diagnosis: Report of a joint WHO/USAI Informal Consultation, October 25–27, 1999." Geneva.

———. 2000b. "A Story to Be Shared: The Successful Fight Against Malaria Vietnam."

———. 2000c. "WHO Expert Committee on Malaria: Twentieth Report." Technic Report 892. Geneva.

———. 2001a. *Antimalarial Drug Combination Therapy Report.* Geneva.

———. 2001b. "Roll Back Malaria, Rapid Urban Malaria Appraisal." Geneva.

———. 2002. "Final Report of the External Evaluation of Roll Back Malaria-Achievi Impact: Roll Back Malaria in the Next Phase." [Retrieved June 7 from www.rbm.wł int/cmc_upload/0/000/015/905/ee_toc.htm].

———. 2003a. *Malaria Rapid Diagnosis: Making it Work.* Geneva.

———. 2003b. *World Health Report 2003: Shaping the Future.* Geneva.

———. 2003c. "Long-lasting Bednets to Be Produced in Africa." *Bulletin of the Wo Health Organization* 81 (10): 776.

———. 2004a. *Malaria Epidemics: Forecasting, Prevention, Early Detection and Contr* WHO/HTM/MAL/2004.1098. Geneva.

———. 2004b. "Report of the Fourth Meeting of the Global Collaboration for Devel ment of Pesticides for Public Health." Geneva.

———. 2004c. "A Strategic Framework for Malaria Prevention and Control during Pregnancy in the African Region." Regional Office for Africa, Brazzaville.

———. 2004d. *World Health Report 2004: Changing History.* Geneva.

WHO (World Health Organization) and RBM (Roll Back Malaria). 2004. *Monitoring and Evaluation Toolkit: HIV/AIDS, Tuberculosis and Malaria.* Geneva.

WHO (World Health Organization) and UNICEF (United Nations Children's Fund). 2003. *The Africa Malaria Report.* Geneva.

Wilairatana, P., S. Krudsood, S. Treeprasertsuk, K. Chalermrut, and S. Looareesuwan. 2002. "The Future Outlook of Antimalarial Drugs and Recent Work on the Treatment of Malaria." *Archives of Medical Research* 33 (4): 416–21.

Williams, H. A. H. A., and C. O. H. Jones. 2004. "A Critical Review of Behavioral Issues Related to Malaria Control in Sub-Saharan Africa: What Contributions Have Social Scientists Made?" *Social Science and Medicine* 59 (3): 501–23.

Wolfe, M. S., J. G. Breman, B. Ainsworth, A.Teklehaimanot, and L. C. Patchen. 1985. "Chloroquine-resistant Falciparum Malaria in Northern Malawi." *American Journal of Tropical Medicine and Hygiene* 34 (5): 847–49.

Wongsrichanalai, C. 2001. "Rapid Diagnostic Techniques for Malaria Control." *Trends in Parasitology* 17 (7): 307–309.

Wongsrichanalai, C., A. L. Pickard, W. H. Wernsdorfer, and S. R. Meshnick. 2002. "Epidemiology of Drug-Resistant Malaria." *Lancet Infectious Diseases* 2 (4): 209–18.

Worrall, E., Rietveld, A., and C. Delacollette. 2004. "The Burden of Malaria Epidemics and Cost-Effectiveness of Interventions in Epidemic Situations in Africa." *American Journal of Tropical Medicine and Hygiene* 71 (2 suppl.): 136–40.

Woube, M. 1997. "Geographical Distribution and Dramatic Increases in Incidences of Malaria: Consequences of the Resettlement Scheme in Gambela, Southwest Ethiopia." *Indian Journal of Malariology* 34: 140–63.

Yamey, G. 2001. "Global Campaign to Eradicate Malaria." *British Medical Journal* 322 (7296): 1191–92.

Yapabandara, A. M., C. F. Curtis, M. B. Wickramasinghe, and W. P. Fernando. 2001. "Control of Malaria Vectors with the Insect Growth Regulator Pyriproxyfen in a Gem-Mining Area in Sri Lanka." *Acta Tropica* 80 (3): 265–76.

Zaim, M., and P. Guillet. 2002. "Alternative Insecticides: An Urgent Need." *Trends in Parasitology* 18 (4): 161–63.

Zaim, M., A. Aitio, and N. Nakashima. 2000. "Safety of Pyrethroid-Treated Mosquito Nets." *Medical and Veterinary Entomology* 14 (1): 1–5.